A CINEMATIC HISTORY of SCI-FI & FANTASY

MARK WILSHIN

CONTENTS

INTRODUCTION

Tales of warring planets, aliens, and robots have existed since the novels of Jules Verne and H.G. Wells in the 19th century, yet it is the science fiction film which has created lasting images of flying saucers and future worlds. From early cinematic dreams of flying to the moon, to nightmares of modern technology, science fiction has recorded the hopes and fears of the human race from age to age. Most popular at times of national and international crisis, science fiction has exposed America's fear of ***communism*** *during the* ***Cold War****, as well as recording each new generation's fear of technology. Yet in order to recreate these imaginary spaceships,* ***cyborgs****, and aliens, science fiction has constantly had to pioneer advances in technology, from early models and miniatures to the modern computerized special effects of today.*

FANTASIES OF EARLY CINEMA

Optimistic about the new possibilities of modern technology, early science fiction films created fantastic visions of the future, with humans mastering the laws of nature and crossing the final frontier into space.

SCIENCE FICTION IS BORN

Georges Méliès' *A Trip to the Moon* (1902) is the most famous silent science fiction film, but it was not the first. In Wallace McCutcheon's *The X-Ray Mirror* (1899), a young woman admires herself wearing a new hat in a shop mirror, before her reflection changes, and she sees herself as a ballet dancer. The film was the first to link science fiction, set-design, and special effects.

GEORGES MÉLIÈS

In 1895, when French magician Georges Méliès attended the Lumière Brothers' première of the Cinematograph, a machine that could project films for an audience, he knew what these films were missing – a story. Méliès saw that he could use film-trick photography and painted scenery in his act.

A TRIP TO THE MOON (1902)

With A Trip to the Moon*, Méliès created the first story in film history. Loosely based on the novel by Jules Verne, it is a comic sci-fi film, where the astronauts are old men in top hats, who fly to the moon in a steel space capsule. Méliès combined the scenes using editing techniques such as stop-motion and lap dissolves, where the old scene fades as the new one appears.*

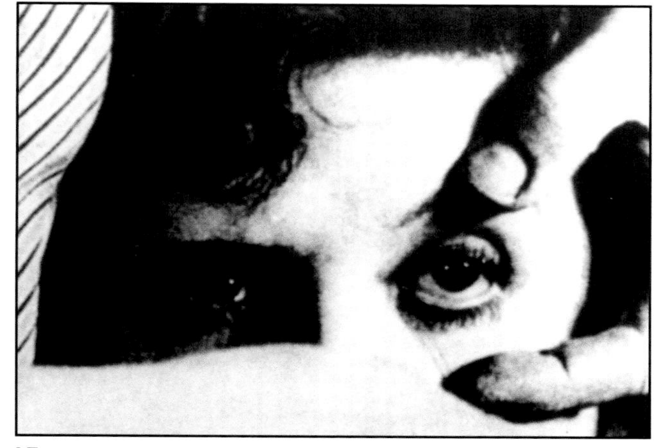

UN CHIEN ANDALOU (1929)

Luis Buñuel collaborated with Salvador Dalí to create a surrealist fantasy. With its seemingly unconnected sequences of a woman's eye being slit open with a knife and a man pulling a piano stuffed with dead donkeys, Un Chien Andalou *has no direct meaning. Viewers decide upon their own meaning as they watch.*

ROCKET SCIENCE

In the 1920s, as air travel was perfected, space travel began to capture the popular imagination and rocket science became the new challenge for the pioneering scientist. Unlike Méliès' comic vision of aristocratic astronauts landing in the man in the moon's eye, Fritz Lang's *Frau im Mond* (1928) gave a more realistic portrait of the science of space travel. With the collaboration of German rocket scientists, Lang showed the journey to the moon in a more realistic way. He included the stage rocket, as well as the effects of acceleration and weightlessness. In this film, it was Lang who used the first rocket launch countdown. Years later, real rockets would launch using a similar countdown.

KING KONG (1933)

King Kong, *the fantastic story of people fighting a giant gorilla, was a welcome escape from the reality of the* ***Great Depression****. Yet it was Willis O'Brien's pioneering special effects that led to the film's tremendous success.*

THE END OF THE WORLD

In the **Cold War** *of the 1950s, the threat of* **communism** *and nuclear war reached its peak, creating a boom in science fiction. This ranged from paranoid ideas of alien invasion to environmental and nuclear disaster.*

THE WAR OF THE WORLDS (1953)

The War of the Worlds *shows the fall of the world's major cities to a Martian army, while scientists race to develop a weapon to defeat them.*

SPACE INVADERS

In 1950s sci-fi films, alien armies were used to represent the threat many people felt from the communist **Soviet Union**, an unknown enemy determined to destroy American values. In *The War of the Worlds* (1953) and *This Island Earth* (1955), aliens intend to take over the Earth, unable to be stopped by an **atom bomb**. This revealed America's fear of losing the race between nations to develop weapons.

ORSON WELLES

Science fiction has been linked to a real fear of alien invasion since the American radio broadcast of The War of the Worlds *in 1938. Welles created panic with a series of live news bulletins in which he read H.G. Wells' sci-fi novel, convincing ordinary Americans that Martians really were invading.*

THE DAY THE EARTH CAUGHT FIRE (1961)

In this film the United States and the USSR launch nuclear bombs at the North and South poles, making the Earth fall off its axis and race towards the Sun. This exposed fears of nuclear arms chaos.

DR STRANGELOVE OR: HOW I LEARNED TO STOP WORRYING AND LOVE THE BOMB (1963)

Stanley Kubrick's dark comedy of nuclear war tells the story of a mad general launching nuclear missiles at the Soviet Union. Three men, a British captain, the U.S. President, and a Nazi nuclear expert Dr Strangelove, all played by Peter Sellers, try to divert the bombs and save the world. The film is making fun of military and political powers, who have created missiles that can destroy Earth.

THE END IS NIGH!

With the atom bomb and nuclear war as a constant threat to society after World War II (1939–1945), there were many Cold War bomb movies. Films like *Five* (1951) and *On the Beach* (1959) show survivors of a **nuclear holocaust,** commenting on society's need to live peacefully. Other films like *Fail Safe* (1964) show how easily missiles could be launched by electrical malfunction, and how Russians and Americans must work to avert war. *Mad Max* (1979) portrays a world of violence, where only the ruthless survive. Other films, like *The Day After Tomorrow* (2004), use global warming as the source of environmental disaster.

THE DAY AFTER TOMORROW (2004)

The Day After Tomorrow *imagines the horror of a new ice age, when New York is torn apart by tidal waves and tornardoes. This is a vision of a future destroyed by ecological threats.*

ALIENS

Aliens have been depicted in many ways during the history of cinema, from the ***humanoid*** *appearance of the first screen alien in* Algol *(1920), to the mucus-dripping frights of the* Alien *series.*

THE DAY THE EARTH STOOD STILL (1951)

An alien and a robot come from space to warn people to stop their nuclear frenzy or the Earth will be reduced to a burnt-out shell.

ALIEN AGGRESSORS

The Thing From Another World (1951) is often considered to be the film that launched the spate of **Cold War** sci-fi films about monsters intent on destroying humanity. It tells the story of an alien spaceship discovered in the Arctic. When the pilot thaws out, he goes on a rampage killing all those in sight.

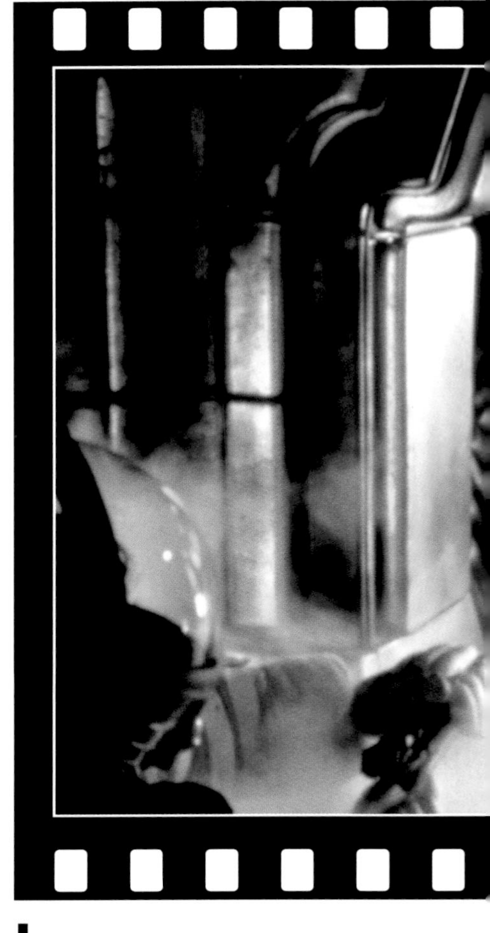

INDEPENDENCE DAY (1996)

This alien invasion echoes the invasion movies of the Cold War, updating them with CGI sequences showing the realistic destruction of U.S. landmarks.

ALIEN (1979)

In Ridley Scott's famous Alien, *a commercial mining spaceship receives what they believe is an SOS message from a distant planet. Upon landing they find a derelict ship, now the breeding ground for thousands of alien eggs. The* Alien *series questions the ethics of colonization and business, while the aliens are depicted as a threat to human biology itself, when a man gives birth to an alien monster.*

E.T. (1982)

Created by sculptor Carlo Rimbaldi, E.T. *is a friendly, 600–800 year old alien, who has accidentally been left on Earth. A young boy befriends him and has to help E.T. get back to his spaceship before he is captured by the police.*

INTERSTELLAR VISITORS

Modern films like *Independence Day* (1996) continued the trend of alien invaders wanting to take over the Earth. However, not all aliens were evil monsters. In *The Day the Earth Stood Still* (1951), the alien Klaatu and his robot Gort are the film's real heroes, delivering a wise warning against nuclear war. As interest in the extraterrestrial grew and UFO (unidentified flying object) sightings increased, so did Hollywood's attitude to aliens, resulting in the incredible supernatural encounters of *Close Encounters of the Third Kind* (1977) and *E.T.* (1982). In *Close Encounters of the Third Kind*, Ray Neary experiences visions after an encounter with a UFO.

MARS ATTACKS! (1997)

A tribute to 1950s sci-fi movies, Mars Attacks! *shows Earth invaded by Martians who have come to destroy it, just for fun. Tim Burton* ***satirizes*** *American society, as his aliens ray-gun everyone from the president to the ordinary citizen.*

ROBOTS

Robots reveal the desire to create life. As technology develops, so does the vision of the robot – from the 1950s box of mechanics to androids, organic machines with feelings and a human appearance.

FORBIDDEN PLANET (1956)

The dressmaking and whisky-producing robot called Robby stands for an optimistic belief in a domestic, mechanical servant.

THE ROBOT REVOLUTION

Making their first film appearance in *The Master Mystery* (1919), evil screen robots later became friendlier in films such as *Forbidden Planet* (1956). As society's faith in modern technology faded, film robots then began to rebel. In *Westworld* (1973) and *I, Robot* (2004), the robots revolt against humans, exposing man's anxieties about living in a computerized world.

BLADE RUNNER (1982)

Ridley Scott's blend of sci-fi and ***film noir*** *presents a dark and grimy Los Angeles in the year 2019, home to androids and humans. Adapted from Philip K. Dick's novel* Do Androids Dream of Electric Sheep? *the film shows the android's desire to be human. As policeman Deckard struggles to maintain his humanity, the film questions what it means to be human.*

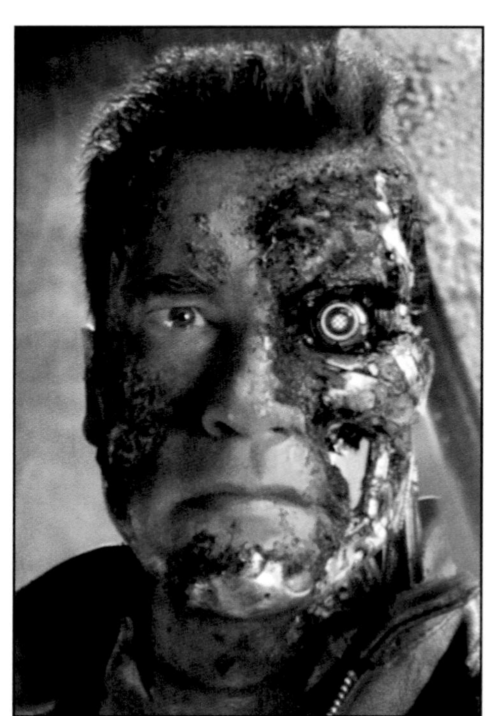

THE TERMINATOR (1984)

Man's fear of the machine – the Terminator is a ruthless ***cyborg*** *sent from the future to kill the mother of a future revolutionary.*

ISAAC ASIMOV

The Russian-born novelist and scientist became one of the most diverse sci-fi writers. He focused mainly on space empires and robots, writing the stories from which Bicentennial Man *(1999) and* I, Robot *(2004) were adapted. Asimov also created* Three Laws of Robotics, *which instruct robots on how to behave.*

I, Robot (2004)

ANDROIDS AND CLONES

Humanoid robots, like the dutiful housewives of *The Stepford Wives* (1975), question discrimination, such as sexism. Films of **clones** and androids, like *Gattaca* (1997) and *Code 46* (2004), where human life is artificially created, make us ask what it means to be human, whether it be human feelings, dreams, or love.

A.I. (2001)

In the dark future of Artificial Intelligence: AI, *the artificial (or 'mecha') boy, David, wants desperately to become a real boy and be loved by his adopted mother.*

SPACE AND TIME

The USA and the **Soviet Union** *were in fierce competition to be the first country to land a man on the moon. For those people caught up in the national* **patriotism**, *films about moon landings and rocket launches were popular crowd-pleasers.*

DESTINATION MOON (1950)

In Destination Moon, *a space mission is financed by U.S. companies, determined to beat the Russians. The film realistically predicted the launch, spacesuits, and the moon landing.*

THE SPACE RACE

In *Destination Moon* (1950) and *Conquest of Space* (1955), space is the final frontier to be conquered, full of drama and exciting machinery. However, when the astronaut Neil Armstrong did make the first moon landing in 1969, films such as *Capricorn One* (1978) and *The Right Stuff* (1983) began to look at some worrying aspects of the space program, reflecting some people's theories that the moon landing was a hoax.

ARTHUR C. CLARKE

A sci-fi author and inventor, Clarke wrote the short story 'The Sentinel' *that inspired director Stanley Kubrick's film* 2001: A Space Odyssey *(1968). They worked together on the screenplay to create a film of outstanding intelligence and beauty that has left viewers puzzled over its meaning.*

2001: A SPACE ODYSSEY (1968)

Based on Arthur C. Clarke's story, 2001: A Space Odyssey *looks at the evolution of humans. Millions of years ago, peace-loving apes find a mysterious stone that begins their existence as violent hunters. Many years later, another stone is found on the moon. Is this the next evolutionary stage for humans? Stanley Kubrick takes a look at the nature of humans – as violent and greedy, and yet capable of change.*

In 1995, *Apollo 13* recaptured the drama of space travel, when a routine flight to the moon became a fight for survival.

TIME TRAVEL

Yet it was not just the science and excitement of landing on the moon that fuelled films about space travel. The possibility of travelling to other dimensions in space and time turned the space film into a discussion about humanity, **evolution**, and the limits of memory.

In *The Time Machine* (1960 & 2002), an inventor is determined to prove time travel is possible. He invents a time machine that sends him 800,000 years into the future where he finds humans divided and fighting one another.

SOLARIS (2002)

In Solaris, *a mysterious ocean on a strange planet is able to materialize a person's dreams and memories, creating an imaginary world more attractive to them than reality.*

H.G. WELLS

Inspired by author Jules Verne's novels of discovery and exploration, Herbert George Wells wrote many sci-fi novels that have been made into films, including The Invisible Man *(1933),* The Time Machine *(1960 & 2002) and* The War of the Worlds *(1953 & 2005). Wells used his novels to look for ways to improve human society.*

BACK TO THE FUTURE (1985)

When Marty McFly travels back to the 1950s in a mad scientist's converted sports car, he must set his parents on the road to love before he misses his opportunity to return to life in the 1980s.

STAR WARS

After the height of the **Cold War** *and the drama of the moon landings, science fiction went out of fashion, only to be revolutionized in 1977 by* Star Wars. *As the sci-fi film evolved into the epic blockbuster, the* **communist** *alien was replaced by Darth Vader.*

GEORGE LUCAS

George Lucas wrote all the Star Wars *films, but he only directed* Star Wars *(1977) from the original trilogy, a series of three films. With the success of* Star Wars, *he set up Lucas Film, which includes the famous special effects company, Industrial Light & Magic. In 1994, Lucas began writing a new trilogy, set earlier than the original, which he then directed.*

STAR WARS (1977)

Droids C-3P0 and R2D2 are mechanical soldiers that land on Tatooine, sent by Princess Leia to tell the Jedi Knight Obi-Wan Kenobi about the Death Star, a space station that can destroy planets. Luke Skywalker, a farmboy, is desperate to escape Tatooine and joins them in their rebellion against the Empire. Obi-Wan teaches him the ways of the force, then Luke enlists smuggler Han Solo and his alien co-pilot Chewbacca to help him free Princess Leia from the evil Darth Vader. Star Wars is set 'a long time ago, in a galaxy far, far away...'.

THE EMPIRE STRIKES BACK (1980)

After Obi-Wan's vision and an attack, the rebels separate. While Jedi Yoda trains Luke, Han Solo and Princess Leia are captured by Darth Vader.

RETURN OF THE JEDI (1983)

The evil Empire constructs a new, indestructible Death Star and the rebels attack. Luke has to defeat Darth Vader to become a true Jedi Knight.

THE EVIL EMPIRE

Unlike some of the 1950s Cold War films, *Star Wars* told its story in human terms, with good finally triumphing over evil. With its fantastic story and incredible special effects, the *Star Wars* trilogy has become an American epic. The first film won six Academy Awards®, along with a Special Achievement Award for the sound effects. For example, the sound of the lightsabre weapon is created from a combination of the hum of a movie projector and a tape of an electrical tower.

SPACE OPERA AND CYBERPUNK

Star Wars (1977) is an example of space opera, a term used to describe early sci-fi adventure stories set in space. *Star Wars* focuses on the action and adventure of inter-galaxy warfare and romance rather than examining the advances in technology. Technology is shown to be grimy and worn, rather than sleek and sparkling, like in traditional sci-fi. With its dark visions of technology running wild, *Star Wars* anticipated the cyberpunk movement, a type of fast-paced sci-fi typified by bleak, futuristic, and high-tech settings.

THE PHANTOM MENACE (1999)

Part of the second trilogy, set prior to the original films, The Phantom Menace *tells the history of characters from the original* Star Wars *films.*

ATTACK OF THE CLONES (2002)

Hollywood's first film entirely shot with digital cameras. Anakin leaves the Light Side of the Force with a spectacular battle between good and evil.

BRAVE NEW WORLDS

In film the future is usually a collage of eye scanners, laser guns, and talking computers, but these technological delights are often just the frills of a nightmare world, where humans are isolated and oppressed by machines.

DARK UNDERWORLDS

From *Metropolis* (1927) onwards, films set in the future have reflected contemporary anxieties about technology and the **totalitarian** state. In *Fahrenheit 451* (1966 & 2005), technology is a state tool to control the masses and books are burned for fear of independent thinking. In the bleak totalitarian society of *1984* (1955 & 1984), love is outlawed and society is watched by Big Brother.

METROPOLIS (1927)

Set in the year 2000, Metropolis *is a divided city, where the rich live in skyscrapers and travel by plane, while the poor scrape a measly living in the industrial city below ground. After several workers are killed in an accident, Metropolis, the tyrant ruler, plans to stop the rebellion by flooding the city, and replacing the workers with robots. Inspired by a visit to New York,* Metropolis *was the model for all cinematic cities of the future.*

PHILIP K. DICK

A prolific writer of science fiction stories, Philip K. Dick revolutionized the genre by setting his tales in the lawless underworlds of the future. He is the author of many novels made into films, including Minority Report *(2002),* Paycheck *(2003) and* Blade Runner *(1982). Dick's stories often question the nature of reality and humanity.*

Minority Report (2002)

SOYLENT GREEN (1973)

Environmental concerns are often projected into the future. Soylent Green *(1973) presents the rise in population as well as global warming and pollution, leading to the extinction of natural food.*

CINEMA AND THE CITY

Since *Alphaville* (1965), future cities have been created using contemporary architecture made to look strange. *Alphaville* made 1960s Paris into a cold, soulless city. Both *THX 1138* (1971) and *Gattaca* (1997) used the Marin County Civic Center, the ultra-modern building of the architect, Frank Lloyd Wright to create a sterile and impersonal future. *Code 46* (2003) shows a divided society, from the modern airports in China to derelict shanty towns in India.

THE MATRIX (1999)

In The Matrix, *Neo, a computer hacker, realizes that his reality is being controlled by a computer and his body is used to power machines. The film shows a world ruled by machines, where human brains are linked to a computer network.* The *film's pioneering bullet-time effect slowed time so that bullets could be seen as they travelled through the air.*

THEM! (1954)

After nuclear tests in the desert, giant ants go on the rampage through American cities. While the army succeeds in destroying the nest, two flying queen ants escape with some drones. The ants have been seen as representing the threat of ***communism*** *to 1950s America.*

MONSTERS

Originating from Jules Verne's science fiction novels of exploration and discovery, films of otherworldly monsters and lost worlds have dramatic adventure that pit the forces of science and progress against the brutal forces of nature.

THE CREATURE FEATURE

Prehistoric monster films like *Journey to the Centre of the Earth* (1959) and *The Land That Time Forgot* (1975) tell of intrepid adventurers and scientists battling through lost worlds.

GREMLINS (1984)

In Gremlins *the sci-fi monster is no longer a potent threat to American society and culture, but rather a comic creature, content with creating mischief and mayhem.*

NUCLEAR NASTIES

As fear of **nuclear power** peaked in the 1950s, sci-fi films about mutated creatures became popular. These mutated animals had been biologically changed, often into monstrous beings. In *The Beast From 20,000 Fathoms* (1953), a man-eating dinosaur frozen for millions of years thaws out as a result of an Arctic nuclear test. The monster starts making its way down the East Coast of the United States, causing mahem. In *It Came From Beneath the Sea* (1955), directed by Robert Gordon, an atomic-powered submarine is attacked by a mutant octopus, exposing the dangerous after-effects of nuclear radiation.

JURASSIC PARK (1993)

*Once scientists discover how to **clone** dinosaurs from fossilized mosquito blood, a millionaire decides to open a theme park. He invites a select group of scientists to inspect his park. But when someone turns the security system off, the dinosaurs escape their enclosures, and suddenly the visitors must fight to survive. Based on the novel by Michael Crichton,* Jurassic Park *became the most successful film of all time at the box office, earning over $120m in just ten days in the United States.*

GODZILLA (1998)

Adapted from the original Japanese movie Gojira *(1954), the giant, mutant monster Godzilla is created by French **atom bomb** testing in the South Pacific Ocean. In a battle between the U.S. military and Godzilla in the streets of Manhattan, Godzilla evokes* King Kong *(1933) and pays tribute to the **Cold War** films of the 1950s.*

WIZARDS & WITCHES

Spells and sorcery do not exist solely in the realm of myth and legend, but can also be found in fantasy films set in the real world, where magic leaks into society from fantasy dreamlands.

SOMEWHERE OVER THE RAINBOW

One of the earliest fantasy adventures was *The Wizard of Oz* (1939). It tells the story of Dorothy, who lands in the magical world of Oz with her beloved dog Toto, after her house is swept up in a tornado.

LA BELLE ET LA BÊTE (1946)

When Belle's father gets lost in a forest, he stumbles upon a castle where he picks a rose for Belle. Suddenly the Beast appears, demanding the merchant's death unless one of his daughters becomes his prisoner. Belle sacrifices herself and falls in love with the Beast. In La Belle et la Bête *(1946), Cocteau creates a magical world where disembodied hands hold candelabras and statues breathe.*

In Oz, Dorothy makes friends with the Scarecrow, the Cowardly Lion and the Tin Man, and together they overcome the Wicked Witch of the West. *The Wizard of Oz is* separated into two sections, with the real Kansas shown in sepia tones, a yellowish-brown tint used in photography, and the fantasyland of Oz shown in bright intense colours.

EDWARD SCISSORHANDS (1990)

In Tim Burton's Edward Scissorhands *(1990) a door-to-door cosmetic salesperson stumbles upon an old mansion inhabited by Edward, a man with scissors for hands. Adopted into her family, Edward adapts to suburban life, cutting hedges and hair. Yet the harmony does not last, as society reveals its prejudice and violence towards the strange and the unknown.*

MODERN SORCERY

Witches and wizards abound in modern fantasy adventures too. In *The Witches* (1990) and the *Harry Potter* series, fantasy is combined with the everyday exploits of children as they uncover the evil plots of wizards and witches. In *Harry Potter and the Philosopher's Stone* (2001) Harry discovers a hidden world of three-headed dogs, elves, and the flying broomstick polo game Quidditch.

JEAN COCTEAU

Cocteau was an artist as well as a writer of poems, plays, novels and films. Focusing on fairy tale and myth, Jean Cocteau created films like La Belle et La Bête *(1946) and* Orphée *(1950). In* Orphée, *the Poet disappears through liquid mirrors into a world where he is part of a risky game with the Princess of Death.*

HARRY POTTER

In Harry Potter and the Philosopher's Stone *(2001), Harry must prevent Voldemort, a murderous wizard at Hogwarts School of Witchcraft and Wizardry, from stealing the philosopher's stone and thus gaining eternal life and the restoration of his power.*

FANTASY, MYTHS, & LEGENDS

Rather than imagining the future of mankind, fantasy films are often rooted in the classical myths of the Greek and Roman ages or Arthurian legends. These trace the adventures of a hero, who battles against the forces of evil in a mystical, magical past.

JASON AND THE ARGONAUTS (1963)

Special effects genius Ray Harryhausen created this fight scene by shooting the live sequence first, with the Argonauts fighting thin air. Then, rubber models of the skeletons were added using stop-motion *(see page 30).*

MYTHIC QUESTS

Based on Greek myth, *Jason and the Argonauts* (1963) is the magical adventure of Jason's search for the mythical Golden Fleece that will give him his rightful place on the throne of Thessaly. On his quest, he must defeat harpies, the giant Talos, a seven-headed hydra, and an army of skeletons.

EXCALIBUR (1981)

Excalibur *depicts Arthur's struggle to become King. With the mystical figures of the Lady in the Lake, the wizard Merlin, and the witch Morgana,* Excalibur *creates a vision of a past age filled with magic and mystery.*

The mythical adventures of Sinbad have also been created on film. In *The Seventh Voyage of Sinbad* (1958), Sinbad has to defeat a cyclops, a giant with a single eye in the middle of his forehead, as well as the giant bird Roc, and a dragon, in order to save a princess from an evil wizard.

THE DARK AGES

Whilst the fantastic adventures of Arthurian legend are based on a mythological past, other fantasy films like *Dragonslayer* (1981) and *Legend* (1985) have created their own enchanted medieval kingdoms, where dragons, unicorns, and demons dwell. In *Legend*, the demonic Lord of Darkness intends to plunge the world into eternal night, by killing every unicorn alive.

JABBERWOCKY (1977)

Based on Lewis Carroll's nonsense poem, the film is set in a medieval fantasyland, where Dennis Cooper must slay the Jabberwock to marry the princess. Bloody visuals help to make it a fairy tale of grime and filth.

LORD OF THE RINGS: THE FELLOWSHIP OF THE RING (2001), THE TWO TOWERS (2002), and THE RETURN OF THE KING (2003)

The ring of the Dark Lord, Sauron, has fallen into the hands of Frodo the hobbit, who must cross Middle Earth to Mordor in order to destroy it. Frodo is accompanied by Gandalf the Grey, Legolas the elf, Gimli the dwarf, Aragorn, Boromir, and three hobbits: Samwise, Merry and Pippin. Peter Jackson's adaptation of Tolkien's novel is a monumental film, examining the nature of humanity and the seductive temptation of power. The trilogy required state of the art special effects, including thousands of digital extras programmed to fight in their own way, to create the tremendous battle scenes.

TERRY GILLIAM

An original member of the comedy team Monty Python's Flying Circus, Terry Gilliam has gone on to make some unique fantasy adventures, including Jabberwocky *(1977),* Time Bandits *(1981) and* Brazil *(1985).*

SUPERHEROES

Freak accidents with deadly waste and radioactive spider bites are normal ways of explaining how comic-book heroes gain their extraordinary superpowers. But in their fight against the world's most evil villains, these superheroes are on the side of the ordinary man.

FLASH GORDON(1936 & 1980)

Football star Flash Gordon fights arch villain, Ming the Merciless, who aims to destroy Earth, and marry the beautiful Dale Arden.

THE SUPERHERO'S WORLD

Superhero films are based on the comic books of DC and Marvel comics. Rather than looking to the future, their imagined worlds often re-create a bygone America, such as Gotham City in *Batman* (1989), based on 1930s New York. Planets from outer space feature in other superhero films, such as the planet called Mongo in *Flash Gordon* (1936 & 1980) and the doomed world of Krypton in *Superman* (1978).

SUPERMAN (1978)

Before planet Krypton hits its red sun, Jor-El sends his infant son to Earth, where his body will become indestructible. The infant crash lands in Smallville, where his adoptive parents teach him about truth and justice. As an adult, he goes to Metropolis, living a double life as a reporter and as Superman, who protects his adopted planet from danger.

X-MEN (2000) and X-MEN 2 (2003)

In a not too distant future, children are born with special powers, after their genes are changed by the X-Factor. A group of mutants, the X-Men, make it their mission to heal the hostility between humans and mutants and overcome discrimination.

BATMAN (1989)

Billionaire Bruce Wayne battles the criminals of lawless Gotham city as Batman. Relying on expensive gadgets, he shows the power of an ordinary man.

MAGIC POWERS

Often the most fantastic element of the superhero film is the origin of the hero's superpowers. In *Daredevil* (2003), Matt Murdoch is blinded by poisonous waste, which then improves all his other senses and gives him a secondary radar sight. Both heroes in *Captain America* (1944 and 1991) and *Hulk* (2003) are transformed by scientific experiments. Yet superheroes are not always invincible. Neither Batman nor *The Punisher* (2004) have any superpowers at all.

SPIDERMAN 1 (2001) and SPIDERMAN 2 (2004)

When outcast Peter Parker is bitten by a radioactive spider, his body genetically mutates, so that he can climb walls and sling webs. During his battles with the Green Goblin and Dr Octopus (above), Spiderman experiences self-doubt.

ANIMÉ

Animé films are, in fact, any animated film from Japan. Yet due to their dreamy nature, many fall into the sci-fi and fantasy category. Their imagined worlds range from cyberpunk, to fairytale fantasy, created by a fusion of hand-drawn animation and CGI techniques *(see page 30).*

SCI-FI VISIONS

Animé films like *Nausicaä of the Valley of the Wind* (1984) and *Grave of the Fireflies* (1988) focus on survival after war and environmental disaster. In *Nausicaä of the Valley of the Wind*, the Princess Nausicaä must bring peace and restore the world's environment by facing up to the truth behind the catastrophic Seven Days of Fire and the mythical Sea of Corruption. Oshii's *Ghost in the Shell* (1995) and *Innocence: Ghost in the Shell 2* (2004), set in the future, look at the **cyborg** soul's dream of becoming human.

FINAL FANTASY: THE SPIRITS WITHIN (2001)

When aliens invade Earth, humans must find a way to destroy them. Using realistic computer-generated imagery (CGI), Final Fantasy *urges for understanding instead of military might.*

METROPOLIS (2001)

Inspired by Fritz Lang's masterpiece, Metropolis *depicts a city where robots live underground and humans live above ground. The film questions what it means to be human.*

FANTASY FOLKLORE

Fantasy animé films look back to the mysteries of Japanese folklore, rich in supernatural creatures, ghosts, and monsters. *Princess Mononoke* (1997) and *Spirited Away* (2001) focus on curses and grumpy gods in a fantasy world of spirits. *Princess Mononoke* has the animal gods of the forest battling against the iron miners who are exploiting their forest.

AKIRA (1998)

Based on the manga comics by Japanese director Katsuhiro Otomo, Akira follows Kaneda, the punk leader of a bike gang through Tokyo after World War III. While Kaneda's friend Tetsuo develops psychic powers, Kaneda discovers Akira, a top secret government project, which could lead to the end of the city. Exposing government corruption and the fear of nuclear holocaust, Akira started a trend for animé in the U.S. inspiring films like The Matrix *(1999).*

SPIRITED AWAY (2002)

The first animé film to win an Academy Award®, Spirited Away *is the story of a girl, Chihiro, who struggles to free her greedy parents from a spell that turned them into pigs. A fantasy world filled with dragons, spirits, and gods reveals the greed of adults and the innocence of children.*

FILM TECHNOLOGY

STOP-MOTION

Stop-motion is a time-consuming method used to animate models or three-dimensional objects by creating a sequence frame by frame, filming one frame before altering the position of the model slightly and shooting the next. The illusion of live movement is then created when the film is projected at normal speed.

TRAVELLING MATTE

In order to create the spaceship battles in Star Wars *(1977) a travelling matte is needed. First, a spaceship is filmed in front of a blue screen, invisible to colour film. Two films called mattes are then created from this, one with a spaceship on, and the other with a spaceship-shaped hole. An optical printer is then used to combine the two mattes.*

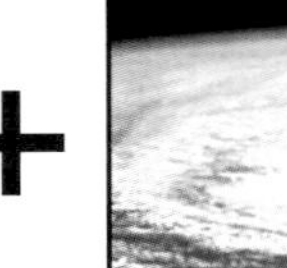

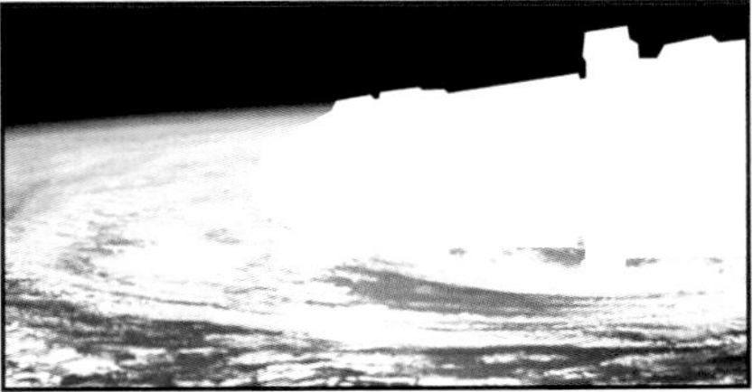

COMPUTER-GENERATED IMAGERY (CGI)

The realistic dinosaurs in Jurassic Park *(1993) were created using CGI. The digital dinosaur begins as a wire skeleton. Layers of texture, such as skin, shadows, rain, and mud, are then added.*

The digital model is then animated by clicking on the dinosaur's different joints. Once animated, the dinosaur can then be added to the live action sequences.

CGI wire model

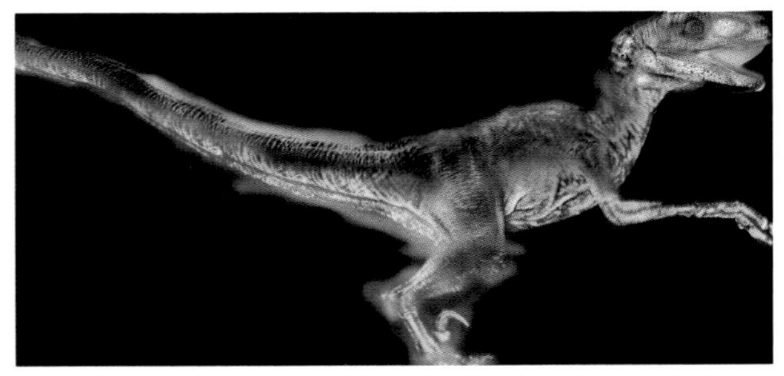

CGI skins

Model ready for animating

GLOSSARY

atom bomb
bomb whose explosive power comes from the smallest part of a chemical element that can possibly exist – an atom

Cold War
state of hostility between nations without an actual war. The term usually describes the situation between the Soviet Union and the United States between 1945 and 1991.

communism
the political theory that class should be abolished and all land and wealth that a country has, shared out equally

cyborg
something that has human biology but electronically-enhanced capabilities

evolution
term used to describe the development of species of animals and plants

film noir
film genre associated with violence and crime. Films are often set in the darkness of night with rainy streets.

Great Depression
the economic crisis in the United States that began with the stock market crash of 1929 and continued through the 1930s

humanoid
having an appearance or character like that of a human

nuclear holocaust
the end of the world as we know it as a result of a nuclear explosion

nuclear power
power, such as electricity produced by nucleur fusion. In sci-fi it is often shown to cause animal and human mutation.

patriotism
term that describes love of your country

satire
when someone or something ridicules another person or thing

Soviet Union
former collection of communist countries that was dissolved in 1991

totalitarian
state ruled by a government that demands complete obedience

INDEX

FILM TITLES INDEX

Table of Contents

Stoddart

Introduction

Picture a beautiful hill covered with trees behind a barn with a rickety fence. Overhead, two hawks wheel and dive against the stormy sky. It is an awesome scene and perfect for capturing in watercolor.

Now imagine this: an exciting urban landscape with buildings, cars, people, streetlights, phone poles, and billboards. Or a dramatic scene of the city lit up at night. How about a train crossing a concrete arch bridge as a jetliner makes its final approach in the sky overhead? These are scenes of everyday city life—a life common and familiar to many of us, and a life that is all around us. A life worthy of documenting in the unpredictable medium of watercolor. In fact, many years ago, the California Scene Painters did just that: paintings of trains, tenement buildings, trucks unloading cargo, and ships entering port. These artists captured something of the fabric of our lives that had rarely been done before: everyday life in the city.

Watercolor is the perfect medium to capture both the peaceful reverie of the country and the gritty chaos of urban life—plus everything in between. This book will help you get started in this challenging and rewarding medium. In it you will find:

- A discussion of materials and supplies for both studio and on-location painting
- Tips and guidelines for painting on location
- Selecting a subject and developing thumbnail sketches and color studies
- The use of photography and how you can work from photos to "say" what you want to say
- The use of a sketchbook both as a planning tool and for final work
- Color properties and relationships and watercolor pigments
- Creating mood with color, changing the lighting and time of day, and painting night scenes
- Keeping your work loose and full of energy
- Adding people and vehicles
- Painting urban scenes, including billboards, phone poles, and signage
- Creating atmosphere with rain and reflections
- Using pen and ink and white paint

At the end of the book, you'll find six step-by-step demonstrations that will help you apply these ideas in a practical way.

My philosophy is based on enthusiastic encouragement and a "you-can-do-it" approach. I want to liberate you from the fear of failure and help you develop the courage to explore and find out for yourself what works and what doesn't. I want you to be able to paint like you were born to paint.

Sunday morning sketch time
out door studio
7/28/06

mini case

sketchbook

A good first sk

children's corner suite – Claude Debussy

GETTING *Started*

Generally, purchase the best materials you can afford. You don't need to purchase a tube of every color or have an arsenal of 30 or 40 brushes. It's better to have a limited number of professional-quality paints and a few good brushes than a cache of lesser-quality tools.

PAINT

TRANSPARENT & OPAQUE

Watercolors come in two types: transparent and opaque. Opaque watercolor is also known as *gouache*, which is similar to the tempera paint you used in school. Gouache contains white pigment mixed in with the color to allow the paint to cover with clean opacity. You can thin gouache and paint with it transparently, if you desire.

Transparent watercolor is what watercolor artists traditionally use. The transparency of these paints allows both the white of the paper and a previously applied color to show through. It is what gives watercolor paintings their luminous glow.

ARTIST VS. STUDENT GRADES

I always buy artist-grade paint over student-grade. Most manufacturers make both. Artist-quality paint flows easier, goes on smoother, and lasts longer than student-grade paint. Student-grade paint contains synthetic substitutes for many of the pigments, and the colors aren't as lightfast as the higher grade. If you can afford artist-quality paint, you will find much more satisfaction and quicker success.

"LIGHTFAST" REFERS TO THE PERMANENCE OF THE COLORS WHEN EXPOSED TO LIGHT OVER A LONG PERIOD OF TIME.

TUBES VS. PANS

Transparent watercolor is available in tubes and pans. Tube paint is similar to travel-size toothpaste tubes and contains paint in soft, squeezable form. Pans are dried cakes of pigment in small plastic cups (or pans). Pans are generally considered best for travel painting, because they are dry and can be transported easily—less mess! Although I have some paint sets that contain pans and occasionally use them, I much prefer tube paint, even for on-location/travel painting. When traveling, I squirt tube paint in my travel palette and let it dry for a day or so, just enough to slightly harden.

It has been my experience that tube paint is fresher and the colors are brighter than pans. It's also easier (and more fun) to paint with. Much of my painting involves scooping big brush loads of paint onto the paper. This is much easier to do with creamy, right-out-of-the-tube paint.

MANUFACTURERS

There are many excellent brands to choose from. I have used Winsor & Newton™, Daniel Smith™, Holbein®, Grumbacher®, Da Vinci®, and Daler-Rowney® with good results. Most recently, I have been using Holbein and Winsor & Newton exclusively. I find their color ranges, consistent quality, luminosity, and brilliance to be in keeping with my goals and direction as an expressive, color-oriented artist. You should experiment with a few brands to find the one that works best for you.

COLORS

This is my current color palette, and these are the colors I used for all the demonstrations in this book. My palette does change occasionally, and yours should too as you experiment and grow as an artist.

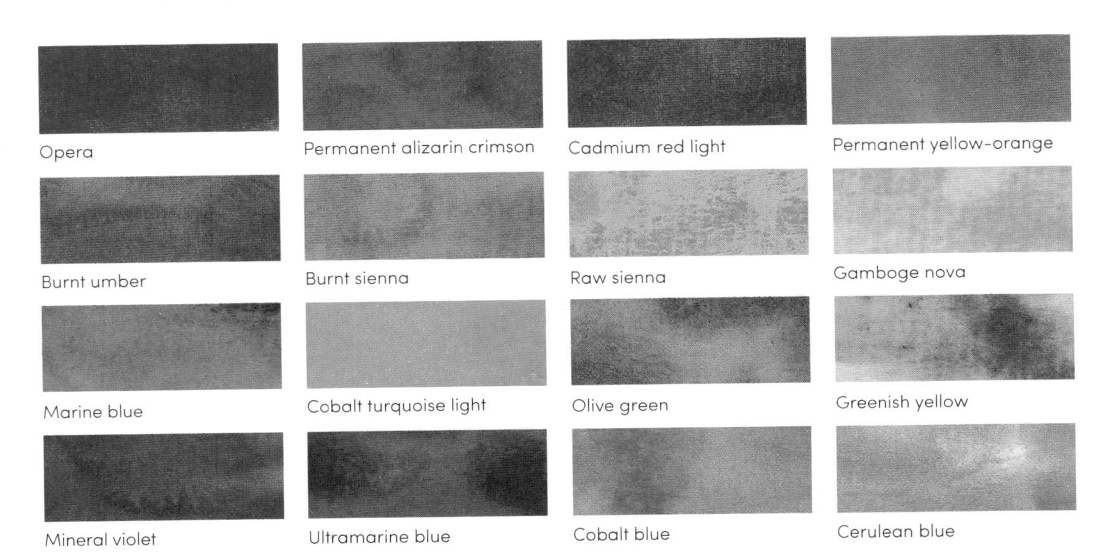

BRUSHES

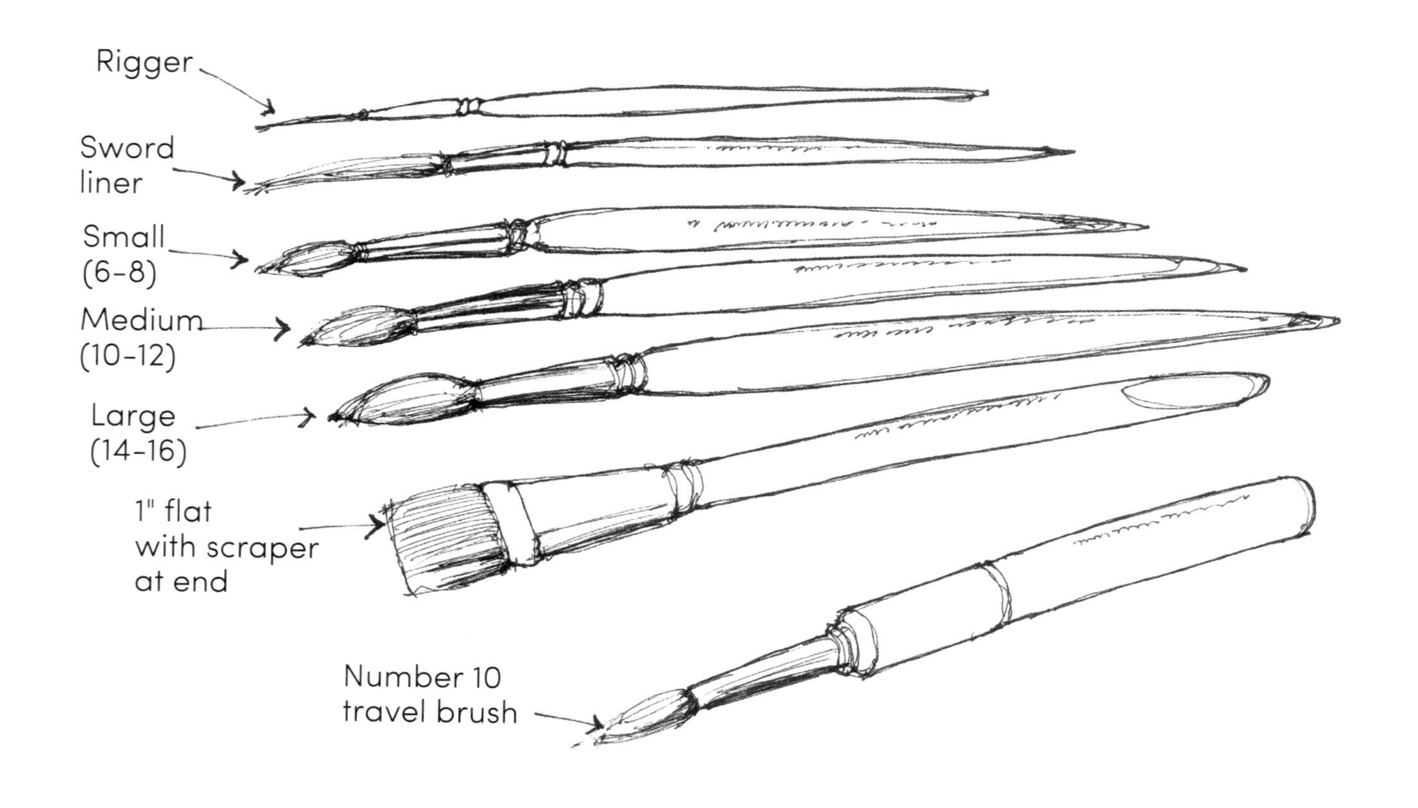

ROUND & FLAT

Brushes come in a wide variety of shapes and sizes. Watercolor artists primarily use two types: round and flat. Rounds are best for general painting. Flats are typically used for wide, generous washes across the paper, although some artists use flats exclusively. I prefer large, round brushes for all my painting.

SIZES

Brushes come in many sizes and are identified by a number, 000 being the smallest and 24 being the largest. Brushes from different manufacturers vary in size—a number 10 from one company may be the same size as a number 12 from another. I suggest you use the largest brush you are comfortable with. This will help you stay loose and avoid painting too much detail.

To keep things simple, I refer to brushes as small, medium, or large. *Small* brushes are between numbers 6 and 8; *medium* brushes are between numbers 10 and 12; and *large* brushes are between numbers 14 and 16.

SABLE & SYNTHETIC

Most watercolorists use either natural brushes (made from animal furs, such as sable and squirrel), synthetic-fiber brushes, or a combination natural/synthetic-fiber brush.

Natural brushes are the most expensive, but they hold a lot of paint and are quite enjoyable to paint with. Synthetic brushes are the least expensive, but they are difficult to control and don't hold much paint. I have found the natural/synthetic combination to be the best blend of affordability and performance. I use Stratford and York Amethyst series brushes and Winsor & Newton Sceptre Gold brushes.

As with everything else, get the best brushes you can afford. You will be rewarded with excellent results.

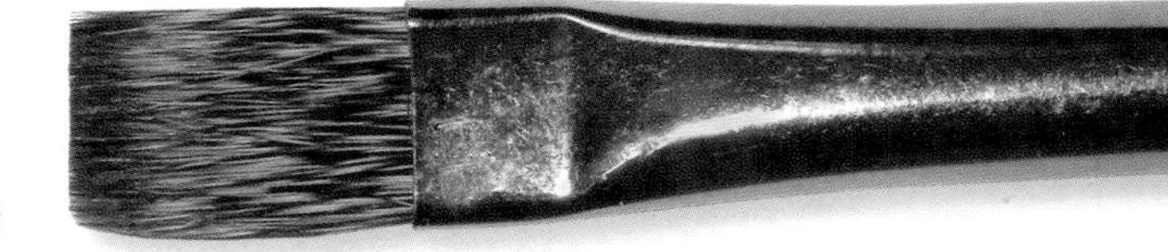

Natural-Hair Brush

Soft natural-hair brushes are made up of the hair of an animal such as a weasel, badger, or squirrel. High-quality naturals hold a good amount of moisture and are an excellent choice for watercolor.

Synthetic-Hair Brush

Soft synthetic-hair brushes are made of man-made fibers such as nylon and polyester filaments. They are an excellent alternative for watercolorists when natural-hair brushes are cost prohibitive. Synthetics are durable and can withstand more use and abuse. Although steadily improving in performance, synthetics do not hold as much moisture and do not have the same "snap" or resilience as high-quality naturals. But remember: A high-quality synthetic is always better than a low-quality natural.

tip

MANY PAINTBRUSHES COME WITH SIZING IN THE BRISTLES TO HELP THEM KEEP THEIR SHAPE. BEFORE USING A BRUSH FOR THE FIRST TIME, RINSE OUT THE SIZING UNDER RUNNING WATER.

TRAVEL BRUSHES

Many manufacturers offer both natural and synthetic travel brushes. These are ideal, as they have a cap that protects them during travel.

CARE

Take good care of your brushes, and they will be with you for a long time.

1. Always immerse your brush in water before dipping it into paint.
2. Never leave a brush resting on the hairs or soaking in water.
3. Clean brushes thoroughly after each painting session.
4. Reshape your brushes after cleaning, and rest them head up in a jar to dry.

PALETTE

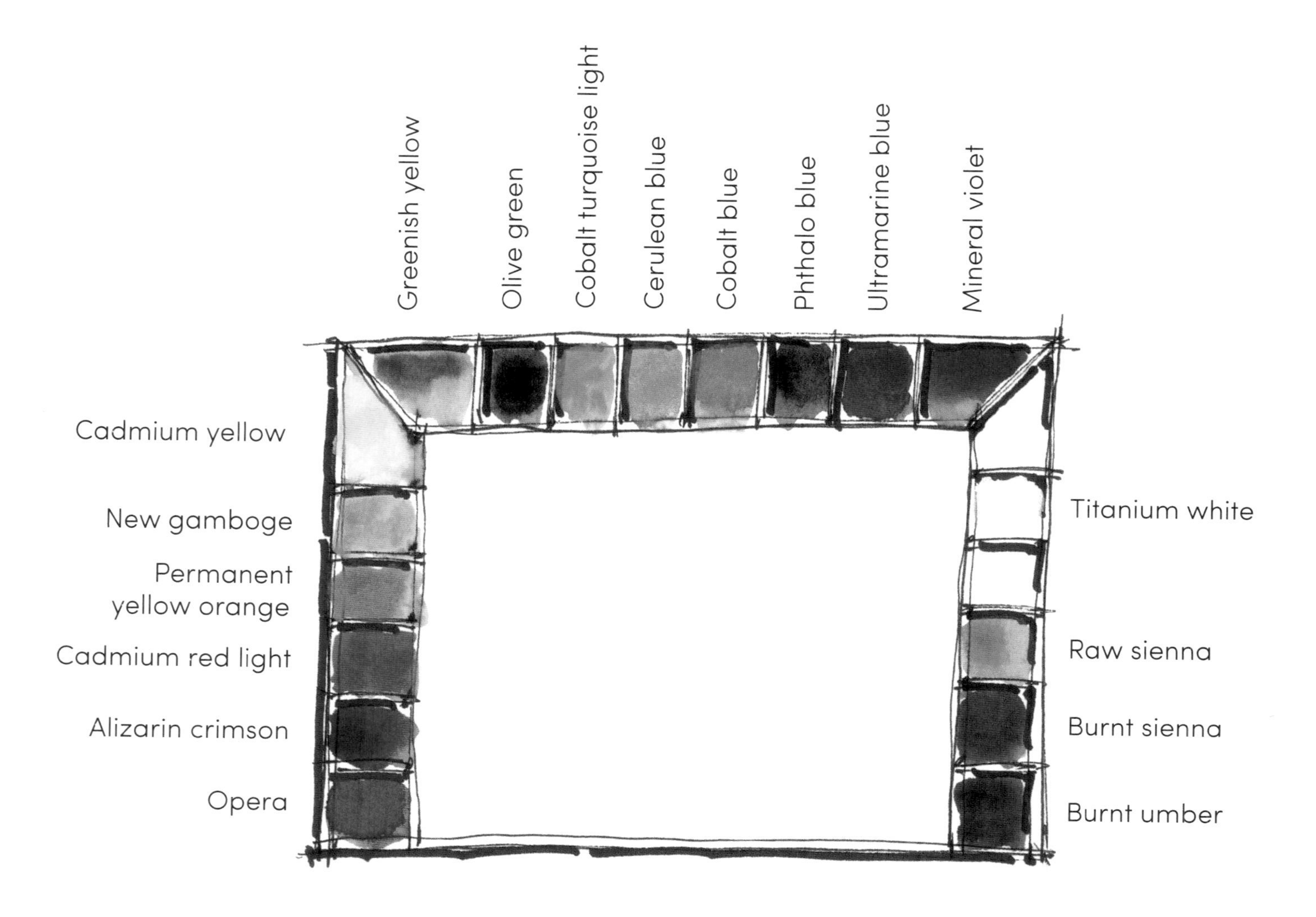

A palette is a flat, shallow container for laying out and mixing paint. It can be as simple as a dinner plate or a metal butcher's pan to a metal or plastic version made specifically for watercolorists.

My studio palette is a Holbein heavy metal palette that is sturdy and very well made. As I like variety, I also occasionally use a John Pike palette, which is a heavy plastic palette that comes with a lid that serves as a place to set your water container and brushes. It also helps keep paint fresh between painting sessions. I keep a moist paper towel in the closed palette.

Be sure to put in fresh color every time you paint; don't squirt in the whole tube and let it dry. I leave paint in the wells and add a little more each time I paint. That way I always have fresh, moist paint to work with. When some of the paint dries, clean it out and put in new paint. You don't want to ruin an expensive brush by scraping out a few cents' worth of pigment from a dried lump of paint.

Organize colors on the palette in spectrum order (like a piano keyboard), so you can learn and remember where each color is. I start at one end with my reds and work around the palette in color-wheel fashion: orange, yellow, greens, and blues. I place my earth tones at the opposite end. When I use white, I place it between purple and the earth tones. Whenever you add a new color, reorganize to make room for the new addition. Don't just plug it in at the end—it's confusing to see a bright red mixed in among greens.

tip

IF YOU'RE UNCERTAIN ABOUT THE ORDER IN WHICH TO LAY YOUR COLORS OUT, PAINT A 1" X 1" SWATCH OF EACH COLOR ON WATERCOLOR PAPER, AND TRIM THEM OUT. PLACE THESE LITTLE COLOR CARDS IN THE WELLS OF YOUR PALETTE IN DIFFERENT ARRANGEMENTS UNTIL YOU FIND ONE THAT FEELS COMFORTABLE.

MASKING FLUID

Masking fluid, or liquid frisket, goes on like thick paint and dries to form a transparent resist on the paper. You can paint right over the masked areas. When the paint is dry, gently remove the mask with an eraser or your finger to expose the clean, white paper underneath.

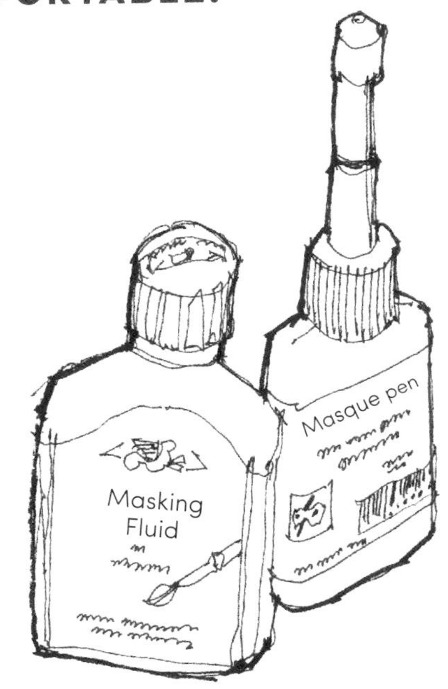

PAPER

TYPES

Most watercolorists use paper made from 100-percent cotton. This paper is referred to as *rag* paper and is archival, meaning it's acid-free and won't discolor with age. Some manufacturers make paper with wood pulp instead of cotton. The surface is a little different but very enjoyable to paint on.

There are three basic finishes: *hot-pressed*, which has a smooth finish; *cold-pressed*, which has a slight texture and is the most common among painters; and *rough*, which is heavily textured. You should experiment with all three to see what surface fits your style best.

Hot-Pressed Paper | *Cold-Pressed Paper* | *Rough Paper*

Watercolor paper comes in three basic weights, or thicknesses: *90-lb.*, which is the lightest and thinnest; *140-lb.*, which is medium-weight and is the most common; and *300-lb.*, which is the heaviest.

I use two types of paper for my work: Fabriano® Artistico 140-lb. bright white cold-pressed paper and Arches® 140-lb. hot-pressed paper.

PREPARATION

I don't soak my paper before painting, because I found that I spent a large amount of time soaking, stretching, and stapling paper, only to ruin the painting within a few minutes, forcing me to start over. I always check the sizing by spraying a little water in one corner of the sheet. If sized properly, the water should remain on the surface for a few seconds before soaking in.

I attach my dry paper to a rigid board, such as Gator board, tempered hardboard, or Masonite, using bulldog clips. The paper will get wet and buckle during painting, but will flatten out as it dries.

Your board should be on a slight incline when you paint to take advantage of gravity, which will help your paints mix nicely on the paper.

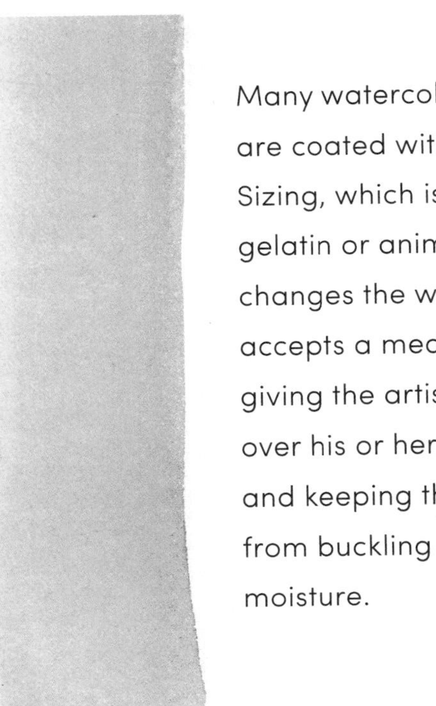

Many watercolor papers are coated with "sizing." Sizing, which is usually gelatin or animal glue, changes the way paper accepts a medium, giving the artist control over his or her washes and keeping the paper from buckling under moisture.

SIZE

I work in two primary sizes: 15" x 20" (half sheet) and 10" x 15" (quarter sheet). Occasionally, I work on a full sheet (20" x 30"), but that is rare, due to the size of my studio and workspace. I have three to four boards of each size so I can work on several paintings simultaneously.

You should paint on the size of paper that you are most comfortable with. You may need to experiment to discover your preferred paper size.

Equipment for the Studio

MAKE A COMFORTABLE WORKPLACE

Some painters have the luxury of a dedicated art area where they can leave their equipment set up. Others must make do with the kitchen table and share their studio with the rest of the household activities. For years, I used my dining table before taking over my garage. Whatever your situation, you want to set up an area for yourself that is comfortable and well-lit and equipped with a basic complement of good art materials.

WORKING SURFACE

I usually work sitting at a table. I have two work lights to evenly illuminate my work area. My palette is on the right—I am right-handed. My water container and paper towel for dabbing are in the lid of my palette. My board is set on a slight incline.

There should be enough room in your workspace to stand back to view your work during the painting process to check for composition, value, and balance.

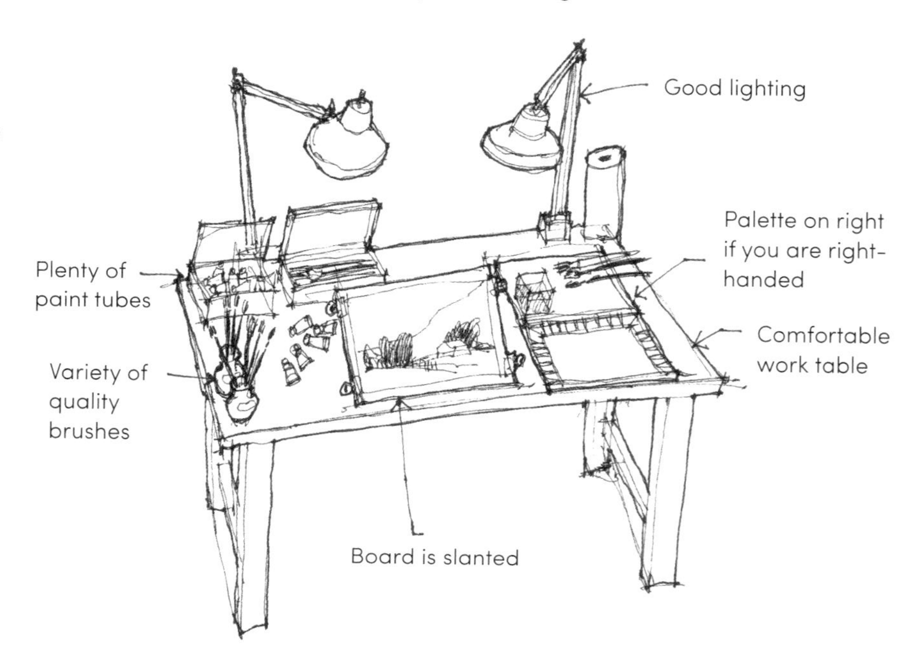

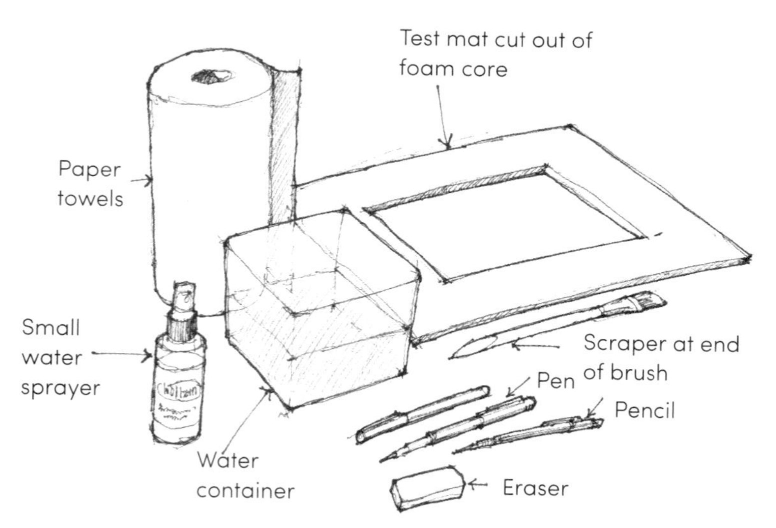

OTHER NECESSITIES

To complete your studio setup, you will need:

- Water container: one that is deep with a large opening
- Spray bottle for keeping your paints nice and wet
- Paper towels
- Pen (I like to use a uni-ball® micro black pen.)
- Pencil: mechanical pencil with 0.9 HB lead
- Eraser (I like to use a Mars® Staedtler® plastic eraser.)
- Scraper tool: the chisel end of a flat brush or a palette knife
- Test mat: for checking composition

Equipment for Plein Air Painting

PACK LIGHT

To me, the most exciting way to paint is on location. Whether sitting outside in your backyard on a cool fall afternoon or waiting at an airport gate, working directly from your subject is the best way to paint. There is an immediacy and directness to your work that is sometimes hard to capture when working from photographs. Your eye-hand coordination is more quickly developed and your sense of "seeing" is further refined.

I bring a complete studio wherever I go, so I'm always ready to paint when the mood strikes or an interesting subject presents itself. The most important thing in equipping yourself for a painting adventure is to keep it simple, and pack light. The last thing you need is a lot of complicated and heavy stuff to lug around. You should be ready to paint within a few minutes.

TRAVELING PALETTE

I have a collection of travel boxes in all sizes, and my preference is the Winsor & Newton Field Sketch Box. This box contains paint, three mixing areas, a built-in water bottle, a water holder, and a small brush. It folds up into a compact travel unit. I replaced the student paints with my own color choices. If you decide to put tube paint in, squirt it in a few days before you travel so it has a chance to harden slightly.

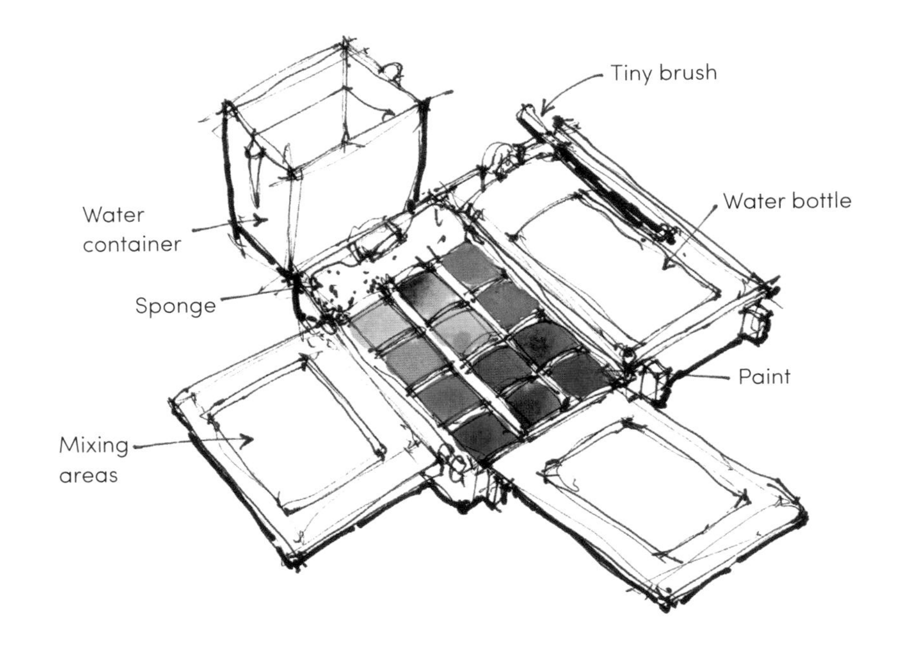

The box has space for 12 colors, so you'll have to edit your master palette. Here is my reduced palette of colors:

- Permanent alizarin crimson
- Cadmium red light
- Cadmium orange
- New gamboge
- Greenish yellow
- Cerulean blue
- Cobalt blue
- Winsor blue
- French ultramarine
- Raw sienna
- Burnt sienna
- Burnt umber

BRUSHES

It's easy to damage your nice brushes in transit, so I use a brush holder. I also always carry some brushes made specifically for travel. They have a built-in protective cap and are available with either sable or synthetic bristles. I have a number 10 and a number 6.

PAPER & SKETCHBOOKS

When on location, I usually work in sketchbooks. I have a variety of sizes and types. For most painting trips, I use either an 11" x 14" Canson® Montval® 140-lb. spiral-bound watercolor book or a 9" x 12" Canson All-Media 90-lb. sketchbook.

In my bag, I carry a 6" x 9" Aquabee® 808 Super Deluxe sketchbook or a Stillman & Birn™ watercolor book, which is perfect for casual sketching and small studies. The paper has a nice tooth and accepts pencil, pen, and watercolor equally well.

Of course, you can always take real watercolor paper with you, but keep it small and simple—a quarter sheet (10" x 14") clipped to a board will do.

EASEL

You can use an official artist's easel, hold a sketchbook in your hand, or do something in between. I use them all. A backpacker's easel (also known as a half French easel) provides a solid support for your work; the only drawback is its weight and the occasional challenge in setting up the wooden legs without pinching your fingers.

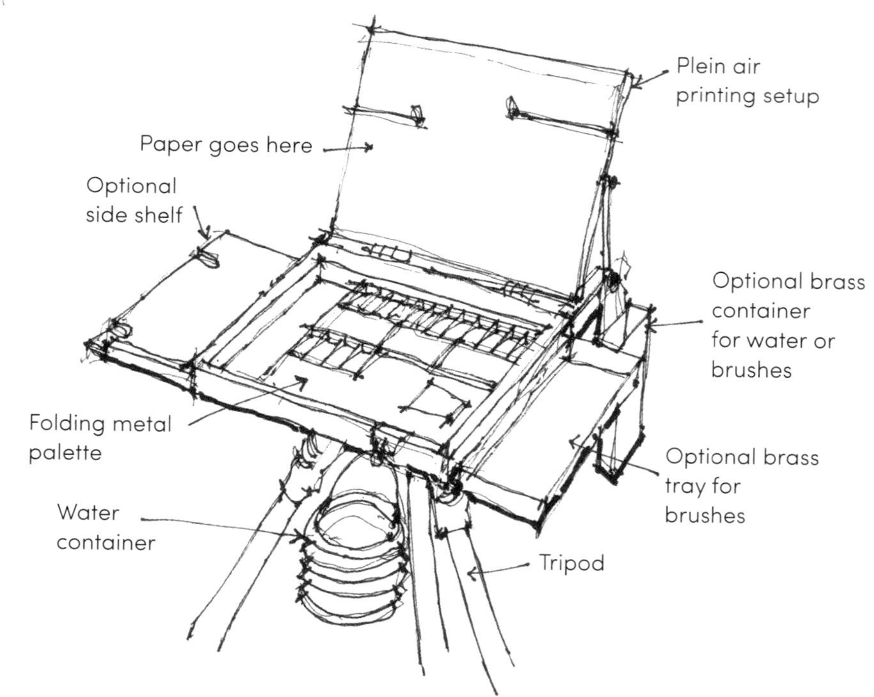

I had a friend attach a block of wood with a threaded Nutsert® to the back of a piece of tempered hardboard (Masonite), which allows me to attach the board to my camera tripod. The paper or sketchbook clips to the board. The swivel head on the tripod allows me to angle the board in any position, from vertical to flat.

Of course, to go super light, just sit on the ground with your sketchbook in your lap!

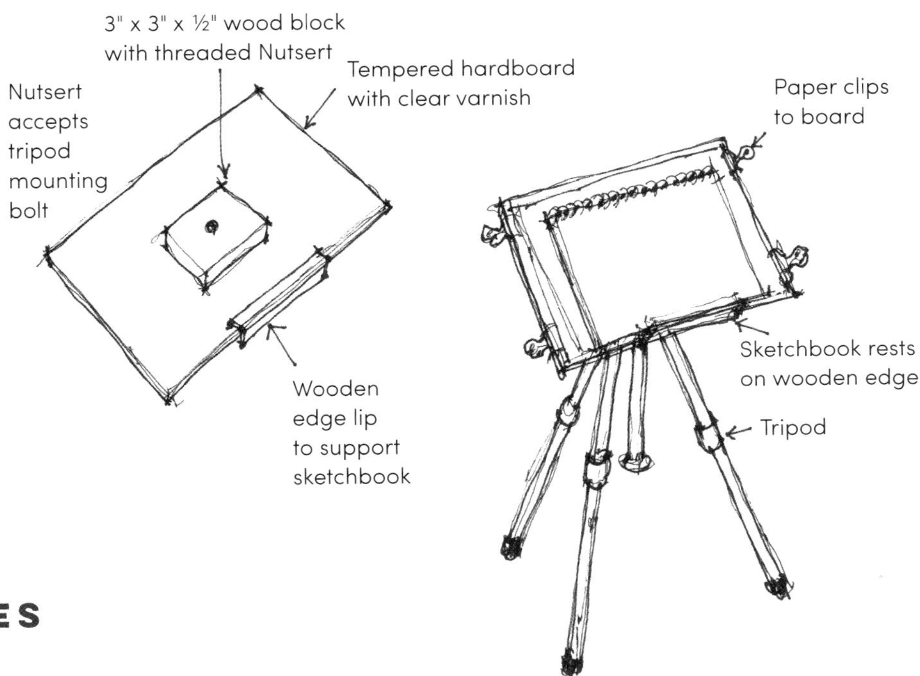

OTHER NECESSITIES

- Water container
- Spray bottle
- Paper towels
- Pencil
- Pen
- Eraser
- Lightweight camp stool
- Small digital camera

LOCATION PAINTING TIPS

- When you arrive, take time to look around and study the scene. Don't be too hasty to start painting. See what attracts you, and then look at it from a few different vantage points.
- Savor the ambience. Smell the air, and enjoy the beautiful colors and sounds.
- Find a comfortable spot with a good view. Although I like talking to people, I try to find a spot off the path and out of traffic.
- After making your thumbnail sketches and value studies, lay in the shadows first. They are constantly changing and it helps to lock them in right away.
- Keep it simple—don't put in too much detail.
- Work fast and loose.
- Learn to read the weather. Your paper and paints will dry depending on the temperature and humidity. On a hot day, keep misting your paints.
- There will be pleasant distractions: a soft fragrant breeze, a dog barking, an airplane overhead, chirping birds, curious people. There will also be not-so-pleasant distractions: heat, a cold wind, rain, an annoying dog that won't stop barking, insects, and curious people. Try to take it all in as part of the experience and roll with it.

PRELIMINARY

Work

Subject & Point of View

Everything starts with selecting a subject to sketch or paint. I suggest that the subject itself really doesn't matter—it's what you do with it that counts. Sometimes the search for that perfect, inspirational scene intimidates us, and we are afraid to start, assuming that our feeble attempts to depict it will fall far short of our expectations. For example, you may love that photo of the Grand Canyon you took last summer. That would make an awesome painting! No doubt it would, but you may want to practice on something a little closer to home to begin with. How about a still life of your art supplies or the wooden bench in your backyard? Such simple subjects can be transformed into beautiful sketches and paintings.

When I think of my favorite watercolors, they are usually of everyday scenes. Yes, I love the epic full-size painting of Yosemite during a dramatic summer storm, but it's the familiar that rings truest for me.

Another aspect of this topic is selecting a point of view that is a little unusual. I love painting an old concrete bridge near my home. It has been under reconstruction for a few years and was covered with scaffolding and surrounded by cranes. The other day I sketched it with all the construction activity going on, and it made an interesting and compelling scene. Here is the simple everyday place, in an unusual setting.

Sometimes I use my camera's viewfinder to explore different views. Better yet, do a series of small, quick study sketches. I often do a few small study sketches before making my large study sketch.

Thumbnail Sketches

A thumbnail sketch is a small, simple drawing done very quickly. I do several of these for each painting, exploring different compositions and value patterns. I try to simplify the scene to make a strong, clear expression of the point of my painting.

I use four distinct values for these sketches: dark, medium, light, and the white of the paper. It's a challenge to work this small, because you must work simply and eliminate the details. This enables you to view your ideas in a simplified, value-only state, creating a strong design-based painting that will look good enlarged. Don't just scribble around; draw in clear, defined shapes. When working with pen, use crosshatching to render the values.

After I have done a few studies of the same scene, I select one that is simple and has a dramatic value pattern. This becomes my "roadmap" for the finished painting. The composition and values are worked out, and I know where I am going. This frees me to explore colors and paint with abandon, following the value study. Sometimes I do one or two larger studies in color, just to explore some additional options. This is another planning tool that helps you practice. Occasionally, I do my study adjacent to my painting, so it's right in front of me as I work. It sometimes becomes a part of the final composition.

Look at the additional thumbnails on the following page. Note how little detail goes into each sketch.

tip

DON'T BE A SLAVE TO YOUR SKETCH. IF SOMETHING ACCIDENTAL HAPPENS AND LOOKS GOOD, GO WITH IT.

Focal Point

A focal point is the part of the painting you look at first. It is also known as the *center of interest.* For most of my paintings, I like to have a clear focal point—a main idea, a reason I did the painting in the first place. Granted, sometimes my main idea is just a beautiful valley bathed in the light of a summer sunset. In that case, the whole painting is the main point.

Most often, however, I want to guide the viewer to something particular in the painting. Good composition usually requires a focal point. There are a variety of ways to do this.

VALUE Place the darkest dark against the lightest light. Your eye will naturally be drawn to that contrast.

COLOR ACCENT Place a bright color in a muted painting.

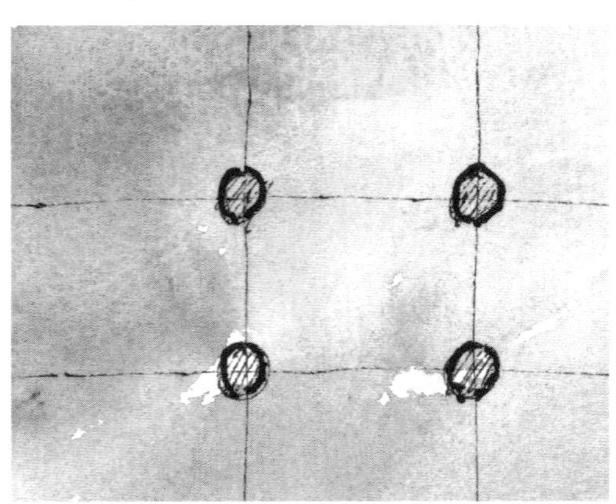

PAGE POSITION Divide the page into thirds, both horizontally and vertically. Where two of those lines cross is where the focal point should occur. Place something of interest (a car, person, phone pole, etc.) there. This is also called the "rule of thirds."

SHAPE CONTRAST Place a smooth-sided object within a background of irregular shapes.

CLARITY Position a defined object within an abstract background.

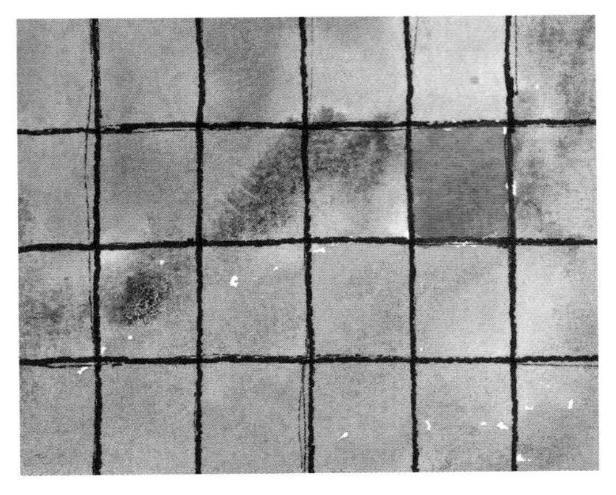

COMPLEMENTARY COLORS Place a red object in a sea of green. (Or a purple object in a sea of yellow, or a blue object in a sea of orange, etc.)

TEMPERATURE Paint a warm-colored object against a cool background.

LINE WORK & DETAIL Include more line work and detail for an object placed within a minimalist and undefined background.

JUXTAPOSITION Place a vertical line in a horizontal painting, or a horizontal line in a vertical painting.

ESTABLISHING THE FOCAL POINT

Avoid using the center of the picture as the focal point. In most cases, the center is the dead zone for object placement. There are exceptions, but for the most part, keep the exact center free of interesting subjects.

tip

IT'S ALL ABOUT CONTRAST. MAKE SURE THAT THE OBJECT IS NOT THE SAME SIZE AS THE BACKGROUND. ONE SHOULD DOMINATE.

Quick Sketching

Whenever the opportunity presents itself, I like to practice quick sketching. The best way to do so is while riding in a car, train, or plane. The goal is to capture the essence of a passing scene in just a few seconds. It's difficult to paint that quickly, so I limit myself to pen-and-ink line-work compositions with a few value notes. I paint them later, relying on my notes and memory for the colors. The advantage to creating a simple line-drawing landscape with no color notes is I can just make something up. Often, those made-up color studies become my favorite little sketches.

I begin with a series of boxes on a page of my sketchbook. Then, as scenes pass by, I look for ones with an interesting shape and composition—something I can grab onto that tells the story in very simple terms.

This exercise trains your eye to find strong, dynamic shapes and lines, and render them immediately. There is no time to thoughtfully ponder and carefully draw. This is action drawing, and it's a nice counter-discipline to the usual approach.

Perspective

The concept of perspective is what gives paintings and sketches depth. The subject itself gives the artist a good start in communicating perspective. A scene with a field, a tree, a house, and a mountain in the distance has a certain sense of dimension, but we can enhance and even force that perception of space and distance by paying particular note to the following:

SIZE For the most part, objects in the distance are smaller than objects in the foreground. This is most obvious when there are two or more of the same object in your scene, such as people or vehicles.

SPACING Objects spaced more closely together seem farther away. Imagine a row of telephone poles next to a railroad track receding into the distance. They get closer together the farther away they are.

LINE WORK Horizontal lines that get closer together as they near the horizon seem to define a recession in space. Imagine the railroad tracks again.

OVERLAPPING Objects in front of other objects give the illusion of distance.

TEXTURE As objects get farther away, their texture becomes softer and less distinct.

DETAIL Objects in the distance have less and more subtle detail.

FOCUS Distant objects are slightly out of focus.

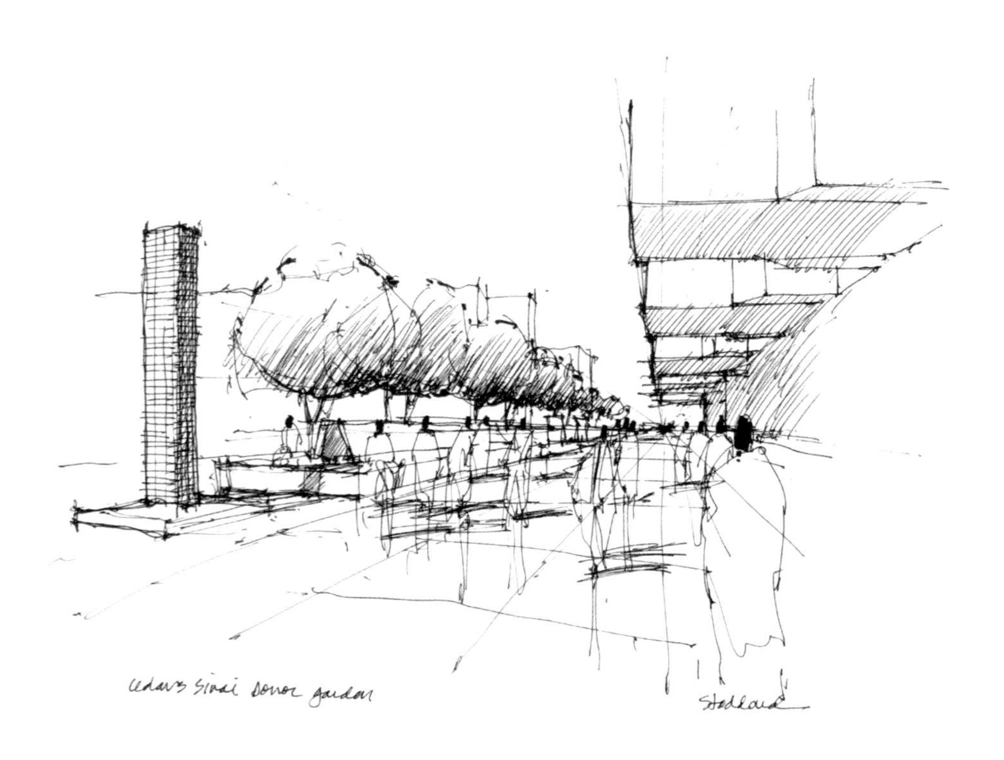

PLACING PEOPLE IN A SCENE

Look at a photograph taken from your last vacation. Notice the people in the scene. Assuming you were standing when you took it, you will see that everyone's heads generally line up with the horizon line. Use this guideline when placing people shapes in your paintings.

ATMOSPHERIC PERSPECTIVE

Color and value can also be used to communicate perspective. Generally, the farther away things are, the more the effects of the atmosphere become apparent. Particles in the air interfere with our perception, which causes loss of contrast, detail, and focus. This is known as atmospheric (or aerial) perspective. Leonardo da Vinci referred to this as the "perspective of disappearance." This phenomenon tends to make objects take on a cooler, blue-gray middle value as they recede into the distance. What does that mean to watercolor artists? Here are a few color notes to remember:

DISTANT OBJECTS

1. Colors are muted and less intense.
2. Colors are cooler.
3. Colors tend to be bluer and grayer, with more middle values.
4. There is less contrast.
5. Shadows are paler.
6. Detail is minimized.
7. As objects recede, they become cooler in tone.

CLOSER OBJECTS

1. Colors are brighter and more intense.
2. Colors are warmer.
3. The lights are lighter and the darks are darker.
4. There is more contrast.
5. Shadows are deeper and richer, with more color.
6. Detail is maximized.
7. Foreground objects are warmer in tone.

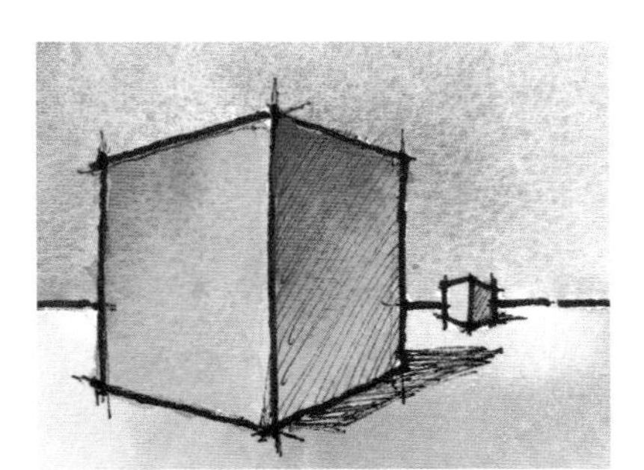

Size *Objects in the distance appear smaller than objects in the foreground.*

One-Point Perspective *Vertical and horizontal lines appear closer together as they move toward the horizon.*

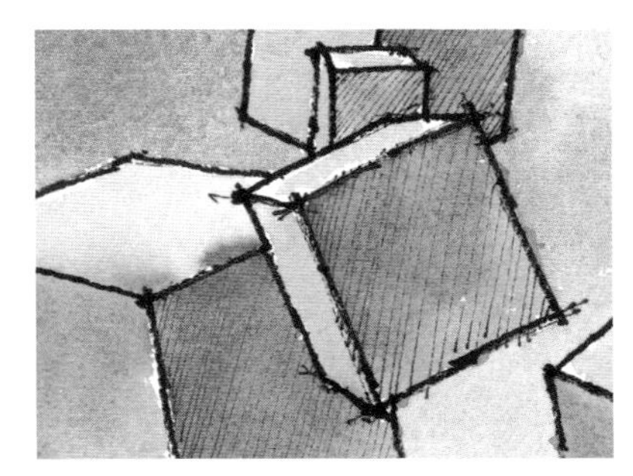

Overlapping *Placing objects in front of other objects helps produce the illusion of distance.*

Detail *Objects in the distance have less detail and appear subtler than closer objects.*

Focus *Objects that are far away appear slightly out of focus.*

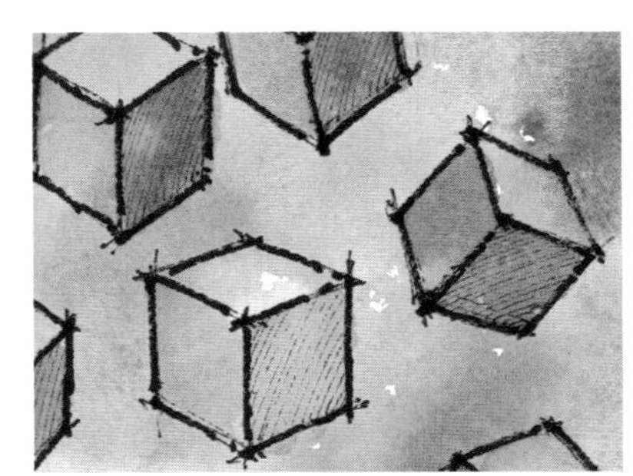

Temperature *Foreground objects are warmer in tone. As objects recede, they become cooler.*

Photography

Photography is a good servant, but a poor master. I don't know who said that, or if anyone did, but I strongly believe it. I love photography. I own—and still use—two film cameras, two digital cameras, and my cell-phone camera. All my paintings are documented both in 35mm color transparencies and digitally, and I have thousands of reference photos and travel slides, all cataloged in carefully labeled notebooks and photo boxes.

I use photography extensively in my painting work as well. Sometime I'm not able to go back to a location to do a sketch or a plein air painting. In those instances, photography is a necessary tool, and I embrace it. I take a quick reference shot after I have completed my study sketch to help me remember any interesting details or color notes. I treat the photo reference as raw material, however, from which I have the freedom to manipulate and modify as needed to express myself more fully.

You should use your own photos if possible. Magazine images are professionally done and may look magnificent, but it's better to use something you have taken that has personal meaning to you. In addition, if you work from someone else's photograph, you should credit the photographer wherever your work may appear and try to obtain permission to use the photo.

Use photos sparingly. If the only paintings I ever did were from photographs, my art would suffer. It would lack dimension, volume, and the sense of the experience of being there. So, whenever possible, sketch from reality.

ARTISTIC LICENSE

As an artist, you never have to paint exactly what you see in your reference photo, or in front of you when painting from life. A dull and lifeless scene might have plenty of potential for an exciting painting, simply by making a few adjustments. You can adjust color or temperature, create dramatic contrast, or even leave out distracting elements. This is taking artistic license, and sometimes it's just what you need to turn a mundane scene or image into an energetic and powerful work of art.

The example on this page illustrates how you can create a dynamic and colorful painting from a traditional photograph.

storm clouds obscure
top of island

KAUAI
bright green

approaching KAUAI

KEEPING A Sketchbook

The Sketchbook

A sketch created in any medium is usually considered to be just a preliminary study for a more substantial work of art—preparation for a "real" painting. To me, however, a sketch has an immediate, raw, pure, and unrefined quality that makes it just as valuable as any other work of art. The sketchbook is an art form in itself. I am always drawn to the loose sketch with notes and thoughts scribbled all over.

Because of my appreciation for sketches, I aim for the same fresh, immediate look in my studio pictures that I achieve in watercolors done on location. Whether working outside or indoors, I sometimes include handwritten notes about the time, place, sounds, and weather within the painting. It's the evidence of my thoughts and feelings and invites viewers to be participants in the experience. They first see the subject through my eyes, and then they add their own interpretation to the parts suggested by loose, painterly brushwork.

I always carry a sketchbook with me, so it's available whenever the mood strikes or I have a few moments to practice. At present, I have completed more than 80 sketchbooks. I sketch and paint everything, from the view from my backyard, to waiting in line at the car wash, to sitting in a train or airport lounge. You don't need to wait for the amazing Grand Canyon view to present itself. Sketch everything.

TYPES OF SKETCHBOOKS

There are many types of sketchbooks. They differ in size, paper type and weight, number of pages, and binding style.

My favorite size is 6" x 9". It's small enough to conveniently carry in my backpack or painting bag, yet large enough for good location sketches and notes. I like a spiral-bound book best. While a perfect-bound sketchbook looks neat, it is hard to use and difficult to edit. It's also much easier to remove a page from a spiral-bound book. Spiral sketchbooks also lay flat and are easy to work with, both on the studio worktable and on location.

I prefer heavyweight paper made for all media, rather than thinner, drawing-only paper. While some of my sketchbook work is limited to pen and pencil drawing, I almost always add watercolor or a similar medium, and you will achieve much better results with a heavier stock.

MEDIA

My traditional drawing tool is a Sanford Uni-Ball pen. It is inexpensive and easy to draw with. I like to paint on location whenever possible, but when time presses, I do the drawing, make a few notes, and complete the sketch later in the studio. I like to use pen, because it doesn't smear if I'm unable to paint it right away.

While I don't use pencil as much, I enjoy the expressive line work a pencil sketch offers. If I want to use pencil but don't have time to paint it immediately, I lay a wash of clear water over the sketch, which seals it and prevents it from smearing.

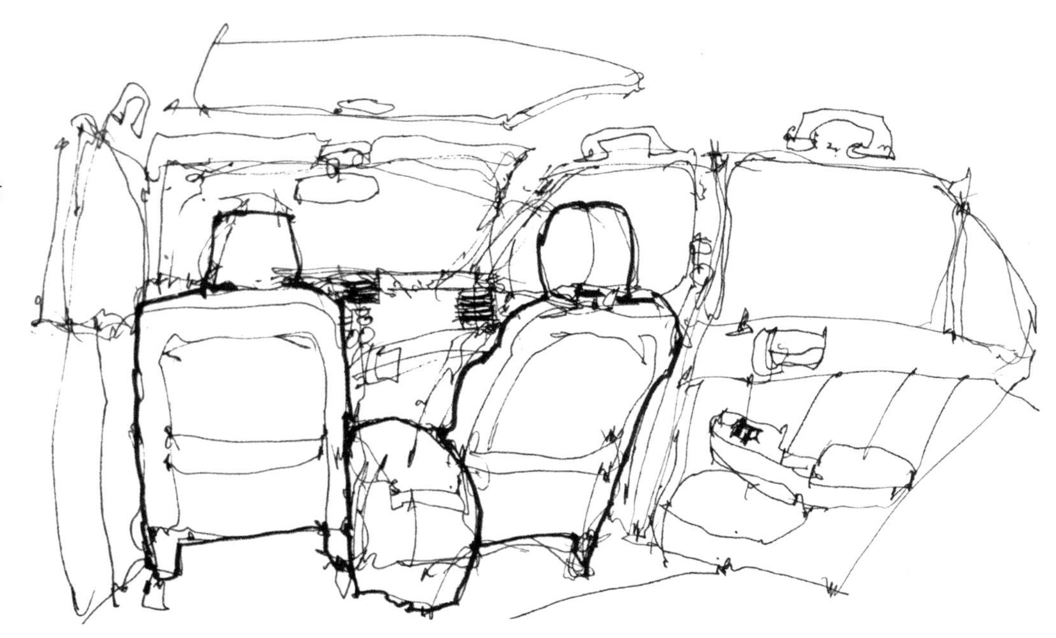

A sketchbook is also the perfect place to experiment with different media. In addition to pen, pencil, and watercolor, I use gouache, watercolor pencils, and pastels. Working with additional media in your sketchbook allows you to become familiar with their respective qualities before tackling a new medium or technique on a full sheet of "real" paper.

PURPOSE

In addition to doing studies for larger works and working out painting problems, you can also use the sketchbook for composition, value, and color studies. Sketching daily helps with eye-hand coordination, seeing a scene, and learning how to translate that scene to a two-dimensional surface.

Taking a sketchbook on trips provides a perfect way to preserve notes and memories, and it's very satisfying to look at a sketchbook from years before and remember your experiences as you documented them. Working in a sketchbook is less intense than "real" painting. You are freer to have fun and not so nervous about wasting materials and time. Finally, developing a collection of sketchbooks is an excellent way to measure your progress over the years.

Guy in a Jimmy Buffet
hat reads a book
8/4/13 7:30 am

PLEIN AIR NOTES

We touched on some of these points in "Getting Started." As most of my sketchbook work is done on location, here are a few more thoughts.

One advantage of living in Southern California is the beautiful weather, and while I can be outside all year round, I particularly love summer. The sun wakes up before I do and stays up well into the evening. I could paint all day if I didn't have to go to work. Sometimes, especially in August, the weather goes a little overboard. It is hot, often smoggy, the sky is hazy, and the air just does not feel as clean and fresh as is does in May. So, what do I do when I don't want to paint outside? I go anyway. No matter how hot or miserable, I go painting. For me, the point of being an artist is to enjoy, experience, and appreciate. There are some obstacles to overcome: the blinding, hot sun that is baking your brain; the occasional breeze that, while cooling you down for a moment, also tends to turn your easel into a kite; the ambient air that heats your paper, evaporates your water, and dries your paints so even the idea of "wet-into-wet" is an impossibility; and finally, those annoying insects that continually interrupt your flow and disrupt your focus. So, what can you do? Here are some suggestions.

1. Organize your painting day so you can paint early in the morning and/or late in the evening—the light is better at those times anyway!
2. Wear a hat and moisture-wicking clothes that will keep you cooler.
3. Rig up an umbrella.
4. Set up in a cool, shady spot.
5. Use bug spray and sunscreen.
6. Travel with minimal supplies, so you don't spend too much time setting up and taking down.
7. Plan on making sketches only. They are small and quick, and you can return home before you get too miserable.
8. Sit in your air-conditioned car and paint. (I think that would still be considered "plein air.")
9. If you are desperate, take a photo, and then work in the comfort of your studio, listening to jazz on the radio, smelling the fragrant incense that you just lit, and gazing out at the August heat from the window.

Whatever it takes, just keep painting.

Drawin
LOS ANGELES JOB CORP

HERALD EXAMINER

Drawing Basics

An artist doesn't have to love drawing to be a good painter, but I think it helps. A good drawing provides a solid base from which to paint, and the more issues that are resolved at this initial stage, the better the chance of a successful painting. I enjoy the drawing process and expressing myself with a carefully drawn contour drawing or a quick gestural sketch—and everything in between.

I use both pencil and pen in my work. Most of my sketchbook work is done in pen for the simple reason that I often don't have time to paint the sketch right away, and a pen drawing usually doesn't smear before I get a chance to add watercolor.

THE PENCIL

When working in pencil, use one with a thick handle and soft lead, such as a 6B. This makes it easy to create three to four distinct values for your study sketch. If the lead is too hard, it's impossible to create good darks, and you run the risk of digging into the paper. When working on site, I use a 0.9 mechanical pencil

THE PEN

When working with pen, I use both waterproof and water-soluble pens. I love the bleed of a pen line when it makes contact with water. It creates nice, unexpected surprises and gives the painting texture and keeps it loose. I have done an entire drawing with water-soluble pen, however, and ended up with a blurry mess with no form or structure to the sketch. My solution is to do most of the sketch with a waterproof pen, and then accent some of the lines with water-soluble pen.

I frequently do a loose, but detailed, pen sketch and leave it unpainted. I do these pen-only sketches for project cover sheets for the design office where I work during the day.

Highly detailed pen sketch

Minimalist pen sketch

WORK SMALL ON THE PAPER

When doing your drawing, make an outline well inside the borders of your paper, and draw within that space. If you are like me and tend to draw larger, this helps you keep the drawing within a reasonable size. It also gives you built-in negative space, in case you want to vignette the painting. Lastly, if the painting gets out of hand from a composition standpoint, white space around the painting allows you to re-crop, if needed.

THE PAINTING IS NOT PRECIOUS

A clean piece of white paper is intimidating. I like to mark up the paper with compositional grid lines before I start. This does two things: (1) it helps me organize the elements from a composition standpoint, and (2) it messes up the pure white paper, making it easier for me to draw on it without fear of making a mess.

tip

I HAVE A PRACTICE MAT MADE OF FOAM CORE, WHICH I CAN PLACE OVER MY SKETCH TO CHECK THE DESIGN AND COMPOSITION.

Color

PARK

Color Basics

I love color and expressing myself with color in my paintings. I never let reality stand in the way of a good painting either. If I think a splash of red would look good in a palm tree, I put it in. A bright purple shadow? No problem! As artists, we are supposed to interpret what is there and express ourselves. Some do it very realistically, while others do it impressionistically.

A fundamental knowledge of color can assist us in clearly expressing what we see and what we want to say. We can communicate feelings, mood, seasons, time of day, and emotions with color. Knowing how colors work and work together is invaluable.

I am a big believer in experimentation. I would rather experiment with different colors than conduct an exhaustive analysis of color theory. A few general concepts are worth mentioning, however.

THE COLOR WHEEL

A color wheel is a visual representation of colors arranged according to their chromatic relationship. The basic color wheel consists of 12 colors that can be broken down into three different groups: primary colors, secondary colors, and tertiary colors.

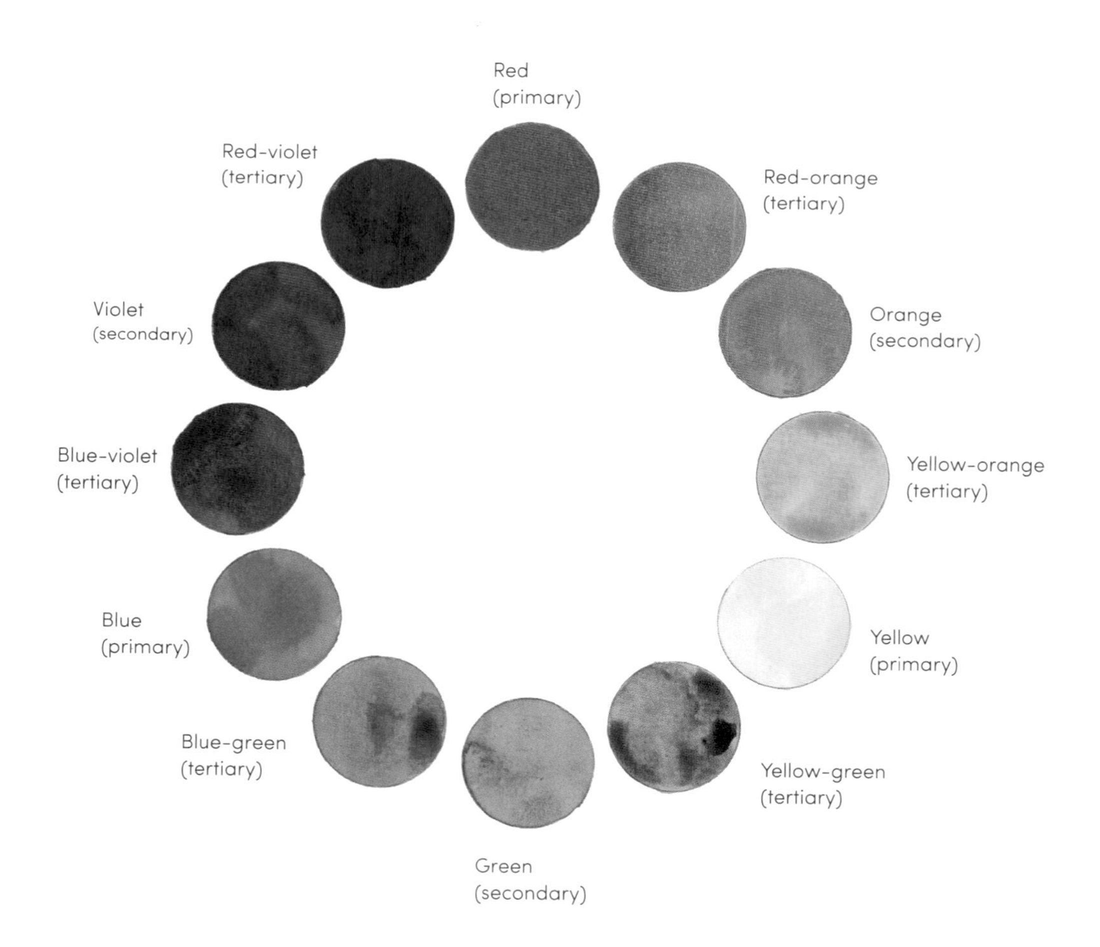

PRIMARY COLORS

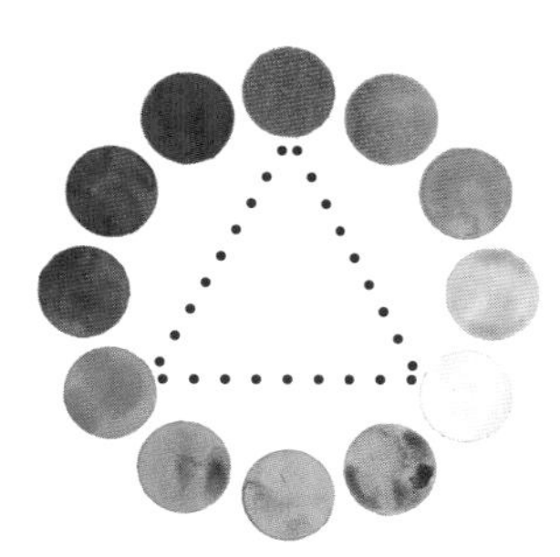

Primary colors consist of red, yellow, and blue. In theory, all other colors can be mixed from these three. They form an equilateral triangle on the wheel. These colors cannot be created by mixing any other colors. The primary colors in my personal palette are a little different than the pure colors of a true color wheel: cadmium red light, gamboge nova or cadmium yellow, and cobalt blue.

SECONDARY COLORS

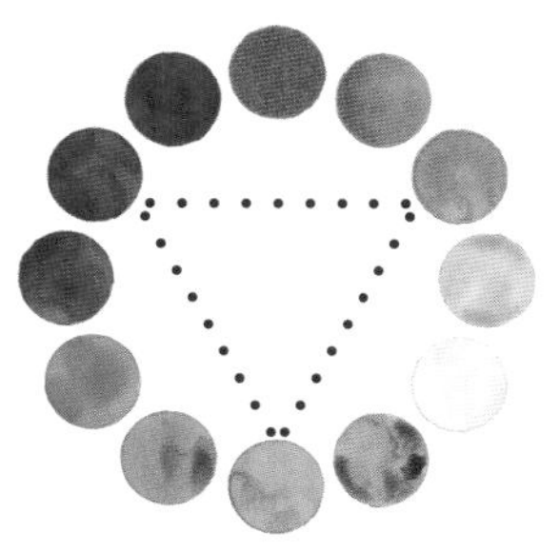

Secondary colors are created by mixing any two primary colors and are found in between the primary colors on the color wheel. Orange, green, and purple are secondary colors. On my palette, the secondary colors consist of: permanent yellow orange, olive green, and mineral violet.

TERTIARY COLORS

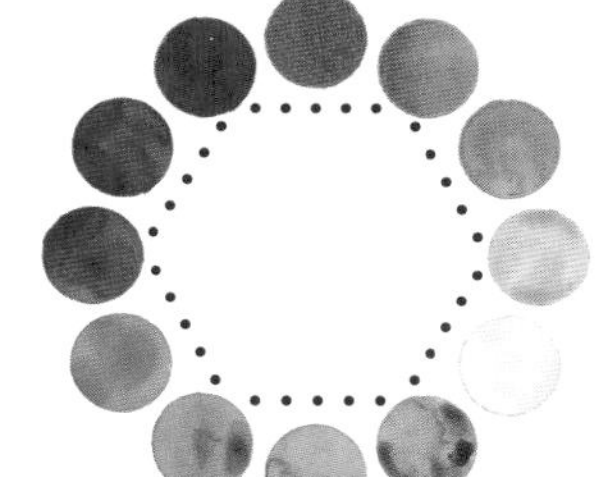

If you mix a primary color with its adjacent secondary color, you create a tertiary color. These colors fill in the gaps and finish the color wheel. Tertiary colors are red-orange, red-violet, yellow-orange, yellow-green, blue-green, and blue-violet. I have to mix most of my tertiary colors, but some come right from the tube:

- Red-orange: cadmium red light + permanent yellow orange
- Red-violet: alizarin crimson
- Yellow-orange: permanent yellow orange + gamboge nova
- Yellow-green: greenish yellow
- Blue-violet: ultramarine deep + mineral violet
- Blue-green: marine blue + greenish yellow

OTHER COLORS

As you can see from my color wheel, I have a few colors outside the circle, although I have located them in the general neighborhood. They are special colors, as you will see in "Special Color Mixes" on page 59.

- Opera: a bright fluorescent magenta
- Cerulean blue: a pale, grayed-down blue
- Marine blue: a brilliant blue-green
- Raw sienna: a warm, grayish yellow
- Burnt sienna: a warm reddish brown
- Burnt umber: a deep chocolate brown

COLOR SCHEMES

Applying a color scheme in your painting can help you achieve unity, harmony, or dynamic contrast. Explore these different schemes to familiarize yourself with the nature of color relationships and to practice mixing colors.

ANALOGOUS

Analogous colors are adjacent to each other on the color wheel. Analogous color schemes are good for creating unity within a painting, because the colors are already related. You can work with a tight analogous scheme or a loose analogous scheme.

Examples of tight analogous color schemes are red, red-orange, and orange; or blue-violet, blue, and blue-green. A loose analogous scheme is blue, violet, and red.

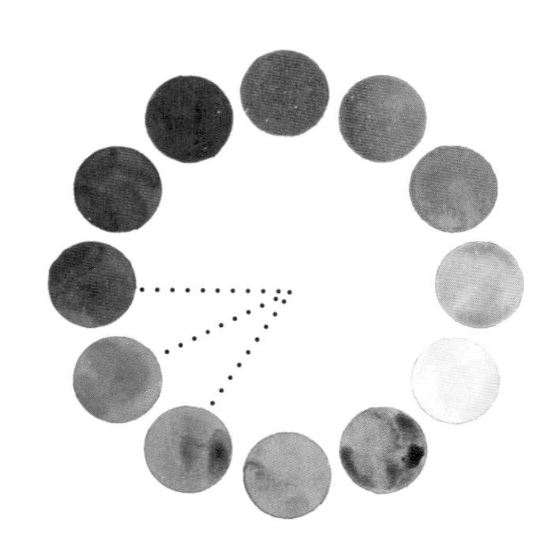

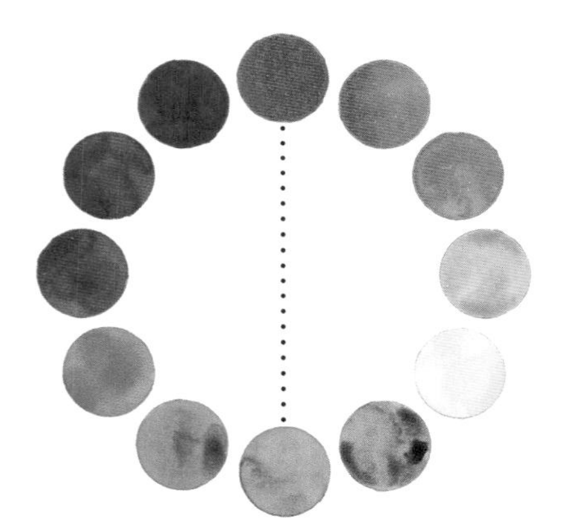

COMPLEMENTARY

Complementary colors are opposite each other on the color wheel. Red and green, orange and blue, and yellow and purple are all complementary color schemes. When placed adjacent to each other in a painting, they make each other appear brighter. They also neutralize each other when mixed.

SPLIT-COMPLEMENTARY

This scheme includes a main color and two colors on each side of its complementary color. An example of this is red, yellow-green, and blue-green.

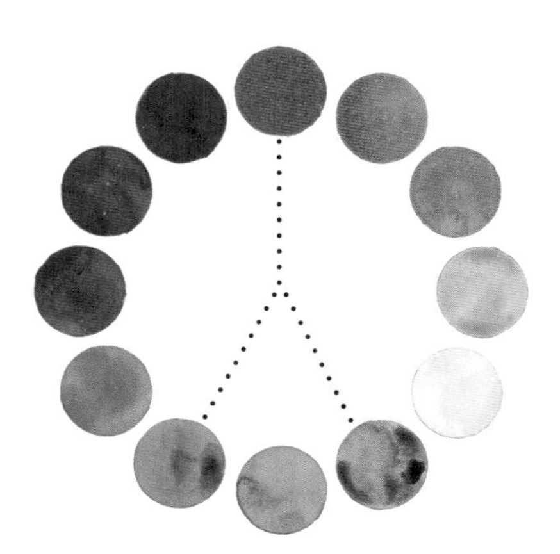

TRIADIC

This scheme consists of three colors that form an equilateral triangle on the color wheel. An example of this is blue-violet, red-orange, and yellow-green.

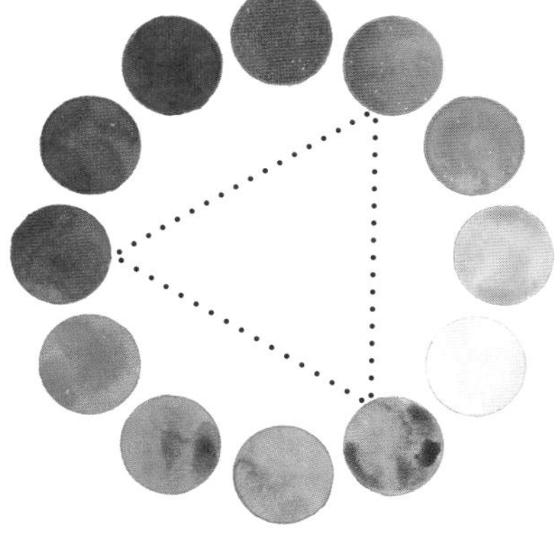

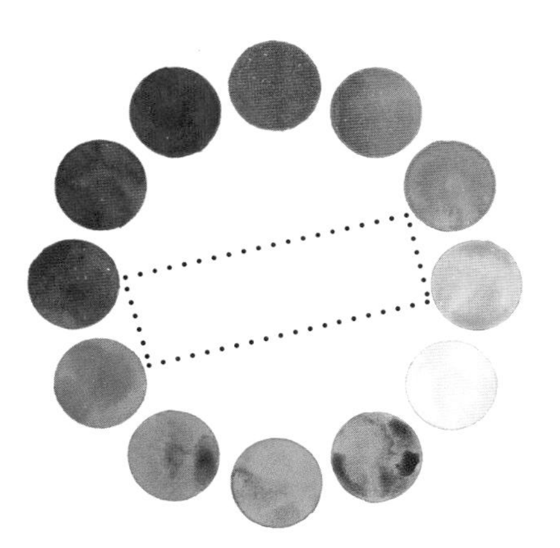

TETRADIC

Four colors that form a square or a rectangle on the color wheel create a tetradic color scheme. This color scheme includes two pairs of complementary colors, such as orange, yellow-orange, blue, and blue-violet. This is also known as a double-complementary color scheme.

COLOR WHEEL REFERENCES

I suggest you make your own color wheel with your own palette of colors. It's also a good exercise to make a complete color wheel using only the three primary colors. This will help you begin to learn about color mixing and how transparent pigments can work together to make new colors.

Color wheel made with three primaries

Color wheel made with primaries and secondaries

COLOR TEMPERATURE

Divide your color wheel in half by drawing a line from between red and red-violet to between yellow-green and green. You have now identified the warm colors (reds, oranges, and yellows) and the cool colors (greens, blues, and purples).

In a painting, warm colors tend to advance and appear more active, while cool colors recede and provide a sense of calm. You can use cooler colors in the background of a painting to help suggest atmosphere and distance.

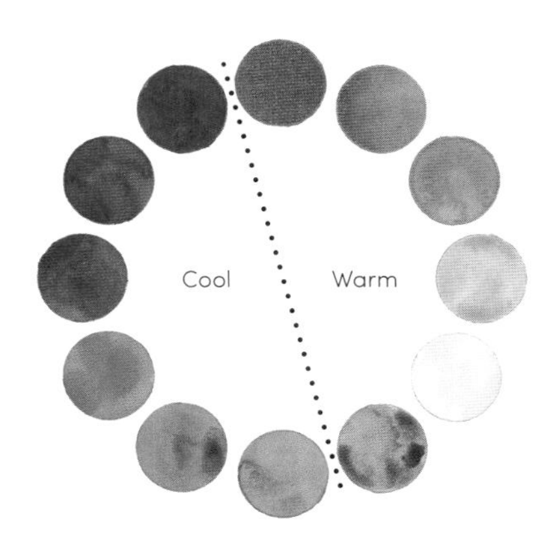

COLOR PROPERTIES

The properties of color are *hue*, *value*, and *intensity*. When you look at a color, you see all three properties. Hue is the name of the color, such as red, yellow, or blue. Value is the color's lightness or darkness. Intensity is the color's brightness or dullness. Let's use blue as an example.

HUE

Hue is the color name. There are many blue hues in our palette. Each one is slightly different. The following are all blue hues:

- Cobalt turquoise: a bright greenish blue
- Cerulean blue: a bright gray blue
- Cobalt blue: a pure blue

VALUE

Value describes how light or dark a color is. Colors have their own inherent values. Squint at a color wheel and you can see light colors and dark colors. You can also change the value of a color by adding white or letting the white of the paper show through, which creates a *tint* (or lighter version) of the color. You can darken the value of a color by adding black or another darker color. This makes a *shade* of the color.

- Ultramarine deep right from the tube is its pure hue

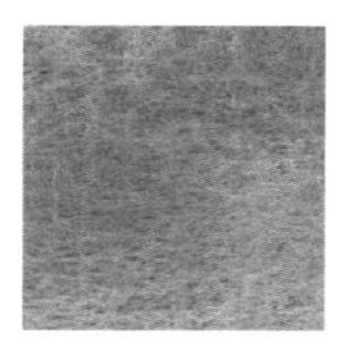

- Ultramarine deep with water added creates a tint (lighter value)

- Ultramarine deep with burnt umber added creates a shade (darker value)

INTENSITY

Intensity refers to the purity (or saturation) of the color. Colors right out of the tube (or as they appear on the color wheel) are full intensity. Adding the complement of that color—or gray, black, or white—neutralizes the color and makes it less intense, or duller.

THE EXCITEMENT OF COLOR MIXING

Painting with transparent watercolors is a unique and enjoyable experience because of the way the colors can be mixed. Other types of paint (oil especially) are typically mixed on a separate palette and applied to the canvas. They are also mixed additively; in other words, white pigment is added to lighten the colors. Transparent watercolor relies on the white of the paper and the translucency of the pigment to communicate light and brightness. A well-painted watercolor seems to glow with an inner illumination that no other medium can capture.

The best way to make your paintings vibrant and full of energy is to mix most of your colors on the paper, *while you are painting*. This is somewhat counterintuitive to the way most of us were taught. In school, you mixed a pool of color in your palette, adding this or that until you reached the correct shade before applying it to the paper. No doubt you created some awesome colors, and there is nothing wrong with this style of painting. I suggest, however, that allowing the colors to mix together on the page, with the help of gravity, creates even more dynamic results.

MIXING ON THE PAPER

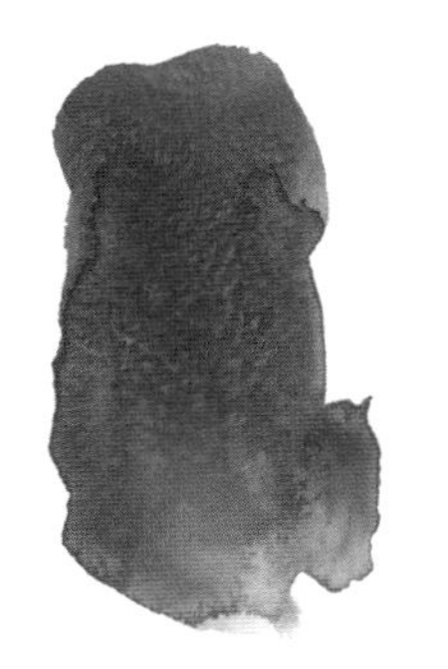

Mix ultramarine blue and alizarin crimson together in your palette until you get a nice, rich purple. Paint a square of color on a scrap of dry paper. Next paint a swatch of ultramarine blue on the paper. While it's still wet, add alizarin crimson to the lower part of the blue wash and watch the colors connect and blend. This is more effective if you slightly tilt the paper. Compare the two swatches. The color and amounts are the same, but the second swatch has the added energy of the colors mixing on the paper.

Now create a dynamic tree color mix. Paint some phthalo blue on your paper. Add some burnt sienna to the lower part of the blue area. Then add some new gamboge to the top of the blue. Watch the three colors combine to make a beautiful tree color.

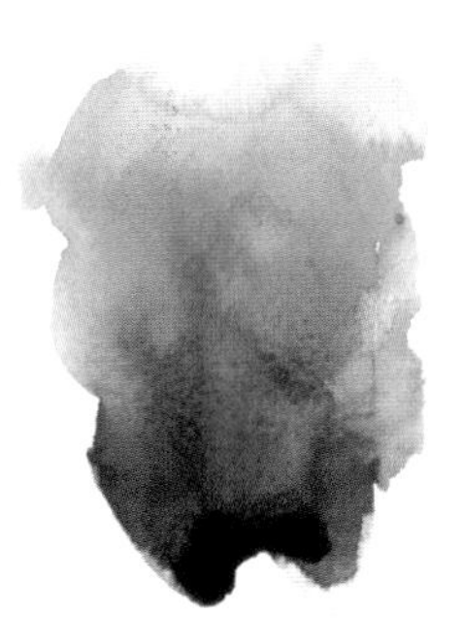

MIXING VIA GLAZING

Glazing is a traditional watercolor technique that consists of applying two or more washes of color in layers to create a luminous atmospheric effect. To paint a sky with glazed washes, paint some ultramarine blue on either wet or dry paper. This first wash is the underpainting, or background wash. Let the wash dry, and then apply a wash of alizarin crimson over the blue. The resulting purple is the result of individual glazes of transparent color.

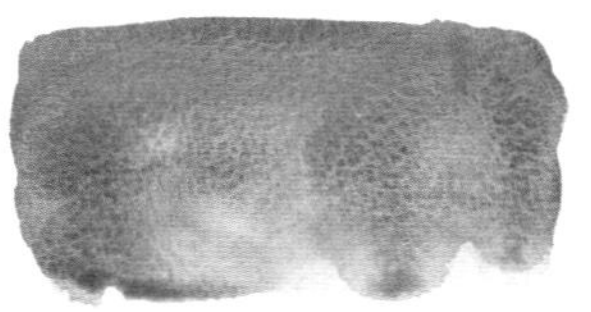

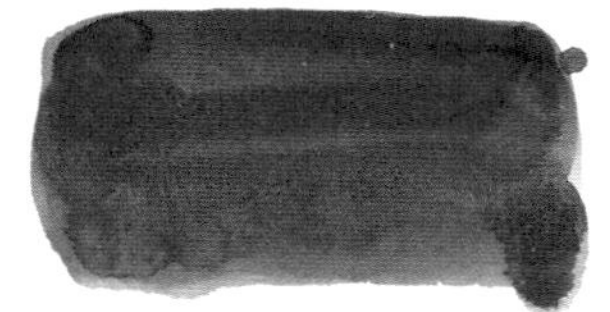

I like to use glazing for sunset scenes and night scenes, using several washes with increasingly more pigment in each one. Glazing unifies the painting by providing an overall background wash of consistent color.

VARIEGATED WASH

To create a variegated wash, paint on wet paper instead of dry. The result is similar to mixing on dry paper, but the wet paper offers a smoother blend of color.

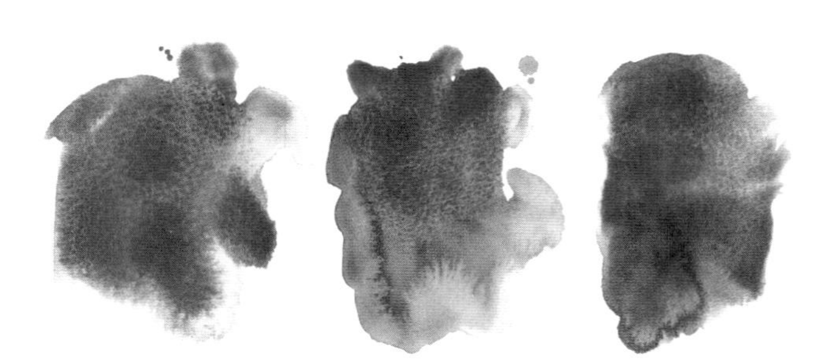

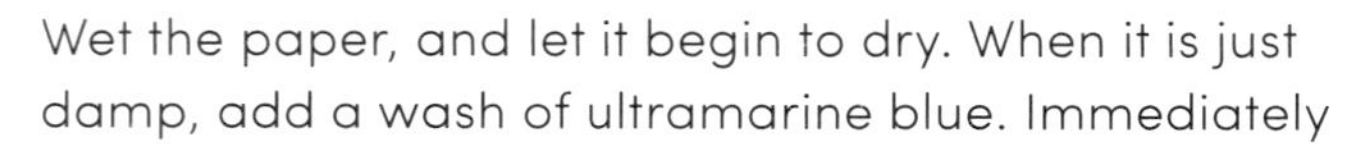

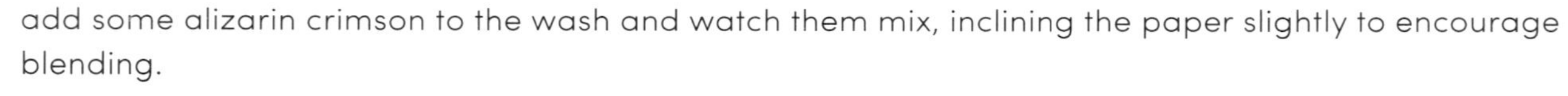

Wet the paper, and let it begin to dry. When it is just damp, add a wash of ultramarine blue. Immediately add some alizarin crimson to the wash and watch them mix, inclining the paper slightly to encourage blending.

WET-INTO-WET

This technique is perfect for painting skies. My skies always have lots of color—and lots of color variation. My wet-into-wet technique is a little unusual in that I don't wet the entire sky area. I dab around a little clear water, loosely following my pencil sketch. This helps create very unexpected and dynamic skies.

Add a small amount of water to a part of your wash area. Add some ultramarine blue to your paper, in both the wet and dry areas of the paper. Now add a different blue. Leave some areas of the paper white. Next add raw sienna and a touch of alizarin crimson. The wet areas of the paper will allow the paint to create a smooth, blended, light wash, while the dry areas will result in a more hard-edged expression of paint.

CHARGING IN COLOR

Charging in color means adding pure, intense color immediately to a wash you have just painted. The moisture in the wash grabs the new color and blends it into itself. This is one of the most fun and exciting techniques to watch—anything can happen.

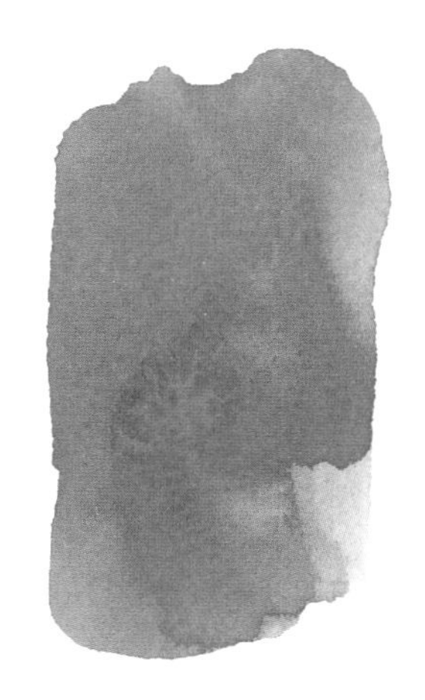

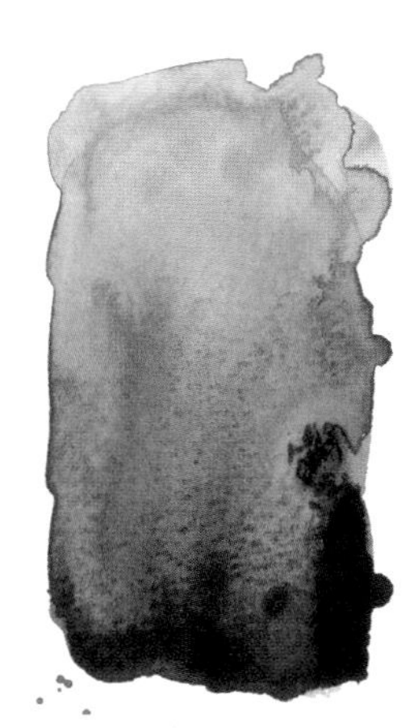

Palette with mud

Palette with distinct colors

MIXING OUTSIDE THE PALETTE

A good way to judge if you are mixing on the paper is to look at your palette after the painting is done. If there are a lot of muddy pools of color, chances are your painting is lacking clear, distinct colors. If your palette still has separate colors in it, good job! You are mixing on the paper.

THE PROPERTIES OF PIGMENTS

In addition to the wide variety of colors we can use to tell our story, the colors themselves have special properties that make for some exciting accidents and unexpected effects. Originally, art pigments came from organic sources (that is, from something living).

Although most pigments these days are synthetic, some still have an organic base. These are the most transparent and express the most clarity of color. Other pigments have a staining effect and are almost impossible to remove once dry, but can be used as an underpainting with dazzling effects. Some pigments are opaque and do not have that lucid transparency the organic pigments have. Other pigments granulate when applied, creating texture as the pigment particles separate.

The point is that different pigments act and react differently as they interact with the paper, water, and other pigments. Try a few of these examples just to get a feel for the paint. Then go paint a picture, and learn by doing and having fun.

TRANSPARENT PIGMENTS

All watercolor pigments are transparent if mixed with enough water. As I mentioned earlier, in this book I'm using *transparent* watercolors, as opposed to *opaque* (gouache or tempera) watercolors. Even within the category of transparent watercolors, some are classified as specifically transparent. These colors are perfect for glazing because they allow the white of the paper and the color from the previous wash to show through. These colors are non-staining and relatively easy to lift off after they have dried on the paper.

Their transparency allows them to be used as a unifying glazing wash over an overly busy painting. Cobalt blue is perfect for this as well as for making luminous shadows across buildings and streets in the late afternoon. Here are the transparent pigments in my palette:

Gamboge

Greenish yellow

Cobalt turquoise light

Cobalt blue

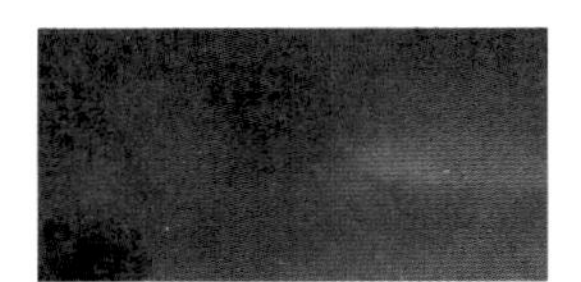
Mineral violet

STAINING PIGMENTS

Staining colors contain pigments that have been ground to submicron particle size. They will stain anything and everything, from your paper to your palette, and can be scary until you get used to them. They are perfect for an initial wash of strong color, because they show through subsequent glazing washes with bright clarity. Here are the staining colors in my palette:

Alizarin crimson

Cadmium red light

Phthalo blue

Opera

WHAT MIXES WELL?

Be extra careful when mixing cadmiums and other opaque colors. They go from pretty to lifeless in an instant. I have found that mixing on the paper allows each color to express its best qualities most effectively. Colors are distinct and brilliant, and you can avoid potentially bad mixes. Use pure color applied to the paper without premixing.

SPECIAL COLOR MIXES

These are some of my favorite mixes, developed over time and many "practice" paintings. The best results are obtained if the colors are left a little unmixed on the paper.

Ultramarine blue + alizarin crimson (deep shadow purple)

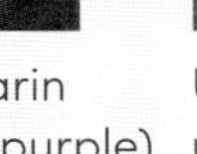
Ultramarine blue + burnt umber (cool/warm gray)

Phthalo blue + burnt umber (cool dark green)

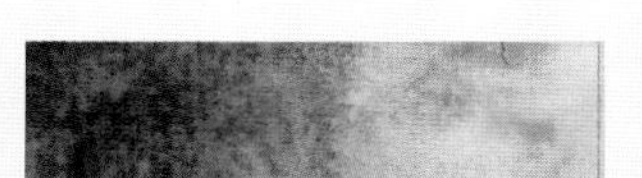
Phthalo blue + new gamboge (bright green)

Cobalt blue + opera (bright shadow purple)

Cerulean blue + burnt sienna (warm gray)

Cadmium red light + new gamboge (orange)

Burnt sienna + new gamboge (brown)

SEDIMENTARY PIGMENTS & GRANULATION

Sedimentary colors contain pigments that have been ground into larger particles than those in staining pigments. The paint particles separate and settle into the valleys of the paper. When this happens, it's called *granulation*, and it's a natural property of some of the denser pigments. Use these colors for showing texture and rawness in an area of a painting. The best examples of this are ultramarine blue and cerulean blue.

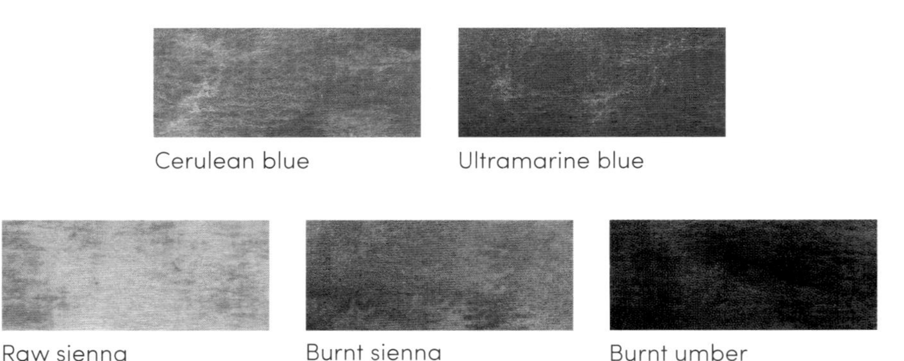

OPAQUE PIGMENTS

Some colors contain pigments that have been ground into very small, densely packed particles that allow little space for the white of the paper or an underpainting of color to shine through. Use these colors to paint over washes of staining colors.

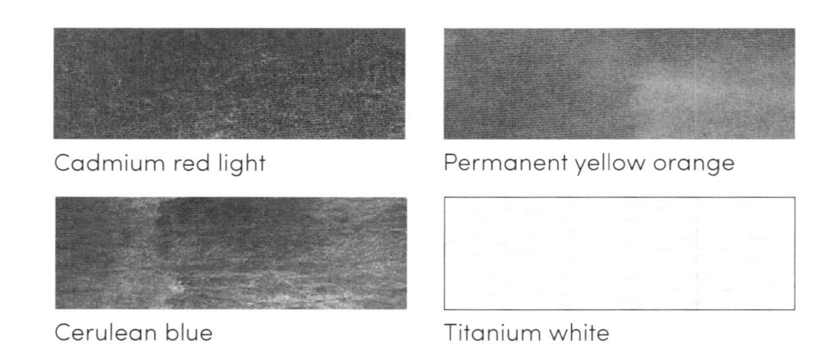

tip

USE CARE WHEN WORKING WITH OPAQUE PIGMENTS. THESE COLORS ARE BEAUTIFUL, BUT IF APPLIED TOO HEAVILY THEY LOSE THEIR BRIGHTNESS AND VIBRANCY AND BECOME DULL, THICK, AND DEAD. OUCH!

CREATING GRAYS & NEUTRALS

I use gray with caution. Most of my paintings are full of bright, pure color. Even my shadows are loaded with color. I suppose I would even put color in a painting of a moody day. And that's the key: lots of color in your grays. Below are a few ways to mix some beautiful grays.

Ultramarine blue + a little burnt umber for a rich, cool gray

Burnt umber + a little ultramarine blue for a warm gray

Cerulean blue + burnt sienna for a different warm gray

tip

WHENEVER YOU WANT TO NEUTRALIZE A COLOR, ADD ITS COMPLEMENT. REMEMBER TO MIX IT ON THE PAPER FOR A COLORFUL NEUTRAL.

You can also mix beautiful grays with ultramarine deep and burnt umber, from cool to warm. Try creating a spectrum chart using these two colors, like the one shown here. Start with pure ultramarine in the first square and gradually add increasing amounts of burnt umber in subsequent squares. The last square should be pure burnt umber.

COLOR & VALUE

I have heard it said that value does all the work but color gets all the credit. I've shared this with all my classes ever since. We respond to the strong values in a painting, but we say, "What a pretty color."

Value is the darkness or lightness of the color. Full-strength gamboge right out of the tube is lighter in value than full-strength mineral violet. We can match the value of mineral violet to gamboge by thinning it down with water, decreasing both its value and its intensity.

For most paintings to be successful, there should be a good *value pattern*, which means a clear and definite arrangement of dark, middle, and light values. These values should not be equal in a painting, but rather predominantly light or dark.

Predominantly light painting

A good exercise is to make a black-and-white print of your painting. Does it read well? Can you see a separation of elements and objects without having to rely on the colors? If so, good job—your values are working for you. Too often we rely on the colors to get the point across, and we are disappointed when that doesn't happen.

Predominantly dark painting

In the example here, I have painted the same scene three times: once with the correct colors and values; once with the correct colors but all the same value; and once with the correct values but wrong colors. Which one makes a better painting? I vote for the one with the correct values and colors.

Correct colors, correct values

Correct colors, incorrect values

Incorrect colors, correct values

WHAT VALUE IS YOUR COLOR?

This chart shows the relative values of each color in my palette. You can tell the value of a specific color by squinting at it. All color drops away, leaving only a shade of gray. Of course, the value of each color lightens when you add water, but this gives you a general idea.

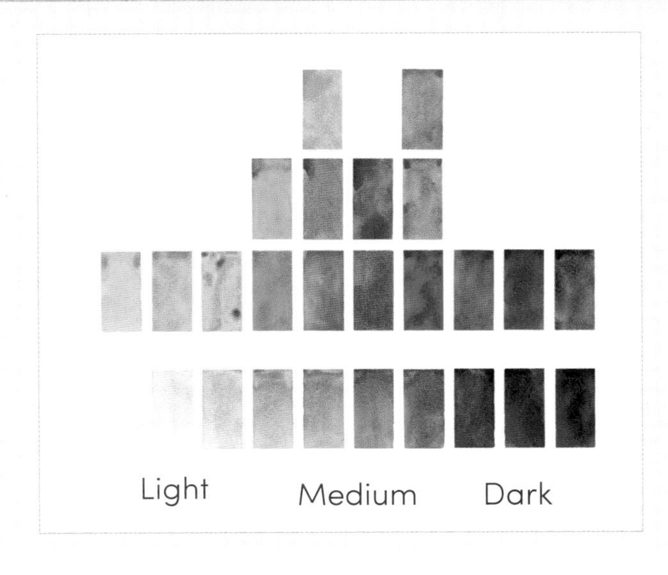

Mission St

Painting

Time of Day

One way to make a painting stand out is to vary the time of day. Most paintings and sketches are done in perfect daylight, perhaps with the sun casting a nice shadow to the left. Changing the time of day alters the lighting dramatically and creates a unique view of your scene. Here are a few examples.

DODGER STADIUM The daytime scene shows a bright green infield with a bold shadow coming across the foreground. The night scene, done from a distance, shows the stadium glowing from within, with a few scattered lights from cars and houses in the background.

UNION STATION The daytime scene is pretty typical: The afternoon sun casts palm tree shadows across the front of the building. The nighttime scene shows light coming from the inside and reflecting on the street, and the trees are lit from below.

COLORADO STREET BRIDGE SUNRISE The landscape is dark, and the sky has just started to lighten. The sun has just broken the horizon.

UNIVERSITY OF REDLANDS AT DUSK Light emanates from the building entrance during an evening event and reflects on the walkway. The sun has just gone down.

COLORADO BOULEVARD SUNSET The sun has just gone down, and the city lights have yet to come on. The sky is still bright.

Urban Subjects

Urban scenes are about texture and the intricate division of space. Pen and ink is a good medium for conveying this. You want to suggest the illusion of detail, rather than actually include it. Be bold with your pen. When you put a line down, do it with confidence. Explore positive and negative shapes.

Add cars, buses, telephone poles and wires, signs, and people—the more the better. Add an airplane in the sky to suggest a busy afternoon. Leave some white space to give the eye a rest and provide contrast to the busyness of the scene. Make colors bolder and brighter than reality, and emphasize the contrast between light and dark. The shadows should be dramatic and full of color. Here are a few examples.

DOWNTOWN LOS ANGELES FROM THE FREEWAY I exaggerated the colors of the buildings and used pen to indicate windows and architectural details. If you look closely, you can see that all the details are mere suggestions. Little touches of white paint give the illusion of detail.

RAINY EVENING DOWNTOWN I used white paint extensively in this scene that depicts a Los Angeles freeway at night. What appear to be building windows and car headlights are just spots of white placed in a grid. Reflections in the pavement suggest rain.

UNION STATION AND SKYSCRAPERS Pen-and-ink is the predominant feature of this sketch. The buildings are painted in bright colors and compressed together in an overlapping graphic pattern. Loosely rendered cars in the foreground draw the viewer into the scene. A small composition study in the lower left adds interest.

CHINATOWN, SAN FRANCISCO The jumble of cars, signs, people, and architecture suggests a busy afternoon in the city. In the distance, sailboats, a bridge, and the shore beyond are suggested with pen and positive/negative shapes.

METRO STATION The Chinatown Metro Station is rendered as a pen sketch, with shadows drawn with crosshatched pen lines. I indicated shadowed areas with solid black pen. When the sketch was complete, I applied bright watercolor, allowing the pen work to communicate the shading and architectural details.

Shadows

Shadows add clarity and depth to a scene. They also suggest time of day and can be used to create drama and mood. Most of us think of using gray or black when painting a shadow; however, I suggest using color. Use a cool mix of cobalt blue and opera or ultramarine deep and alizarin crimson. Paint the shadow shapes first, and add the wall color afterward. For shadows across green grass, use a mixture of marine blue and burnt sienna.

Exaggerate the length of the shadow along the ground, especially across the foreground. This suggests late afternoon. It also frames the subject and directs the eye upward.

When painting white walls, use the same color for the underpainting for both the walls in shadow and the sky. This integrates the elements and unifies the painting.

Remember to be consistent with the light direction, so all shadows come from the same place. Here are a few examples.

VISTA DEL ARROYO The afternoon sun casts a soft shadow across one wing of this building. I used a combination of opera and cobalt blue to capture the luminous quality of the light. I painted the shadow color first, and then painted over it with raw sienna for the wall color once dry.

HUNTINGTON LIBRARY I used a similar treatment for this building as in the previous example, except that the wall color is left white. The bright green grass and dramatic shadows across the foreground help communicate the feeling of late afternoon.

PASADENA CITY HALL In this painting, the shadow treatment is subtle. The building to the left is in shade, indicated with my traditional purple mix. There are some shadow streaks across the front of the building, caused by the trees in front, and the archways are also in shade. I left part of the dome unpainted to suggest a glinting highlight; by assumption, this dictates the shadowed side of the tower. The people on the stairs create slight cast shadows.

SIXTH STREET BRIDGE, LOS ANGELES The shadows really make this sketch. They angle across the bridge support and project onto the river channel in the distance and across the grassy area in the foreground. The strong value contrast between the highlight and shadow tells you it is a bright, sunny day.

LIBRARY STEPS, LOS ANGELES Most of this scene is in shadow, caused by an adjacent skyscraper. The clue that it's in shadow is the highlight on the steps in the lower left of the sketch. A mix of cobalt blue and opera is perfect for illustrating cool shade.

Vignette

Often, what isn't painted is just as important as what is. Leaving white (or negative) space around or within a painting helps the eye focus on what is important. Explore vignettes in the study sketch phase, and learn to appreciate what isn't painted.

One effective technique is to do a detailed pen-and-ink sketch in the center of the page, gradually showing less detail as you work outward. Then, when painting the sketch, put color in the center only, letting the outer parts of the sketch remain unpainted. Here are a few examples.

WATER TROUGH, SOUTH PASADENA In this sketch, I left out the background completely, allowing the viewer to appreciate the structure and tree without additional distractions.

HILLSIDE HOUSES This very small sketch was done quickly with pen and a few simple colors. Houses and trees overlap in a composition held together by the interesting shapes it creates and the use of negative space.

OLD PASADENA STREETSCAPE This started out as a pure pen-and-ink line drawing. The perspective and composition were good, but it lacked a pulse. I added soft colors to the center of the scene, moving outward to create energy and movement. Painting the entire drawing would not have been as interesting, so I left it partly done.

BACKYARD BUILDINGS, KEELER This painting illustrates a very minimal vignette approach. The painting is full of color and value, but it fades out along the right side to keep the eye where the dark and light values and complementary colors converge.

PACIFIC SURFLINER A light vignette keeps the eye toward the center of interest. Placing buildings and other elements in the background would distract from the central theme of the piece.

Reflections

Reflections add energy and color to a scene. They can suggest an afternoon rainstorm or help make the foreground interesting.

Paint reflections at the same time you paint the object. If there is a passage of dark green trees, paint the mirror image directly below. Make some horizontal strokes through the reflection to suggest the flow of water and the irregularity of puddles. On a city street at night, the reflection will extend farther than the height of the object.

This also works for painting lakes. If the reflection is distinct, the water is calm. Busy water will have broken bits of color. Here are a few examples.

CITY STREET, SOUTH PASADENA This simple scene of a street and railway crossing is enhanced and made more interesting by the addition of a colorful reflection that fills the foreground. I took many liberties with shape and color, using the excuse of a reflection to pump more color into the scene. The horizontal strokes through the color help communicate water and enforce the perspective.

SANTA FE DEPOT As this is an extremely horizontal subject, I used both the background trees and the foreground reflections to introduce some verticality. These reflections are subtle and abstract, rather than literal and tight.

EVENING RAIN, LOS ANGELES

A rainy nighttime scene is the perfect subject for exploring reflections. The taillights of the cars on the freeway create bold streaks of red. At the center of the painting, lights from the distant buildings reflect onto the freeway. Don't worry about accuracy. Rather, go for a feeling of excitement, and express colors boldly.

OLD PASADENA AT NIGHT One of my favorite settings is Old Pasadena on a rainy fall evening. Cars heading down Green Street create bright red reflections that extend to the bottom of the page. The yellow light from store windows is also reflected, as are the shapes of the pedestrians braving the weather.

LOS ANGELES RIVER In this placid scene, the Los Angeles River acts as a mirror, reflecting the banks, concrete structure, and dark trees behind. A spark of sunlight peeks through the trees. Even though this is a direct reflection, I enhanced the colors in the river, introducing opera and cobalt blue, just to jazz it up a bit.

Trees

The logical way to paint a tree is to start with a trunk, add some branches, and finally populate it with a hundred leaves. It never really looks quite right this way, however.

A better approach is to paint trees with shape and value. Refer to your value and composition sketch, which shows you where the dark masses of trees are. Paint the tree mass with an initial wash of dark at the bottom and shadow side, and follow with brighter values at the top, letting the colors mix. Use negative painting to outline brighter trees in front of darker ones. As the paint starts to dry, use a chisel tool and short, quick strokes to scrape out trunks and branches.

Exaggerate the value difference between the dark and light areas to create drama and interest. Using a rigger with both white and dark paint, paint dark branches against a light background, and light branches against a dark background.

Where the tree connects to the ground, continue the trunk color to the side to suggest a shadow. This connects the shadow to the trunk and integrates the tree with the landscape. Here are a few examples.

GREEN STREET, PASADENA In this city scene, the collection of trees bordering the street is painted as one large shape, with a shadowed side and a highlighted side. The fact that there are multiple trees is indicated by the rhythm of trunks marching into the distance.

PINE TREE SHADOWS, COLORADO This little study sketch is dramatic, due to the strong, dark value of the foreground pine tree and how it envelops the meadow. I used a fine-pointed brush to paint the boughs, with some random scraping to suggest detail. I suggested the distant aspen trees by painting the background with yellow and dark green, leaving the trunks light.

ARROYO SECO PATH In this scene, a mixture of light and dark values with selective scraping indicate highlights, shadows, and volume.

PALM TREES, LOS ANGELES PARK This sketch illustrates how lack of detail can still communicate trees. Loose, organic shapes painted with a variety of colors indicate the palms: yellow, green, blue, and red. The dark undersides of the palms extend down to form the trunk. The high contrast between the foreground and background trees helps communicate depth. Notice how the trunks blend into the strong cast shadow on the grass.

Skies

The key elements in painting an exciting sky are shape, value, and color. Use a wide variety of color in the sky: blue, purple, red, yellow, white, gray, and brown. Watercolor makes painting skies easy—they practically paint themselves!

Even on a clear day, I might use three blues: ultramarine deep, cobalt blue, and cerulean or cobalt turquoise light. Alizarin crimson provides a nice warm accent, as does raw sienna. For cloud shadows, mix ultramarine deep with burnt umber for a rich, cool gray. For a dramatic sky, paint a dark mix of gray and blue next to an unpainted area. Experiment by applying clear water in random areas of the sky.

Remember: Leave some white space, don't overpaint, mix on the paper, allow room for accidents, and let gravity do the rest. Here are some examples.

SUMMER SKY, KAUAI In this quick sketch, I used a light touch and plenty of water to suggest soft clouds in a blue sky. I limited the sky colors to cobalt and ultramarine.

WINTER AFTERNOON, COLORADO The winter sky in Colorado is clear, fresh, and pale blue. In this scene, it is late afternoon and the sun is easing toward the horizon. I used raw sienna and gamboge nova, fading to a mixture of cobalt turquoise and cerulean blue. I kept the washes light to allow the paper to show through to give it a feeling of warmth.

EATON CANYON SUNRISE I left the paper unpainted to indicate the sun and surrounded it with a light wash of raw sienna and gamboge nova, fading into ultramarine blue, cobalt blue, and opera. Notice how the sun actually looks bright.

MOUNTAIN AND STORM CLOUDS This stormy sky is clean and bright, with distinct areas of color and value. Cerulean and ultramarine blue applied directly to pure white paper without mixing, as well as bold applications of ultramarine with burnt umber, suggest a quick summer storm coming over the mountain.

AFTERNOON STORM, COLORADO A dark and stormy sky dominates this landscape. Note that the clouds look darker because some of the sky is pure white, and there is a white edge between the blue sky and the clouds.

People

Adding people to a scene is a great way to infuse life and energy into your painting. I am a great proponent of "blobular-shaped" people. These forms are made with a single dab of the brush, followed by a tiny dot for the head. The looser these forms, the better. I have seen many beautiful paintings ruined by overworked, overdetailed, stiff people.

I like to use bright accent colors for my people, preferably in a complementary color to the background. When painting a group, let the colors run together from person to person.

When painting people by themselves, make a pen-and-ink contour sketch before adding bright colors and patterns. Leave the highlights unpainted. Here are a few examples.

FAIR OAKS PHARMACY Loose, organic shapes that vaguely look like people bring life to this scene. The looser, the better—just keep in mind the scale and perspective. I try to keep everyone about the same size to avoid confusion.

LOS ANGELES STREET SCENE The people are mere suggestions in this sketch: small dots for the heads and body shapes that fade to nothingness.

CAFÉ DU MONDE, NEW ORLEANS A line of abstract shapes in spectrum order, positioned in front of a dark background with occasional splashes of white paint, clearly suggests people gathering at a café.

AIRPORT WAITING ROOM In this impressionistic scene of an airport waiting room, the man in the foreground has a little detail, while every other passenger is rendered with loose lines and shapes.

RESTING MAN The strong red color of the shirt, working in concert with the dark background, makes this little study interesting and dramatic.

Vehicles

As with people, vehicles add interest to any urban sketch. They are an excellent way to add an accent color. Like when painting people, I have found that simpler is better.

One technique is to paint a horizontal shape with a tire extending down from each corner, two thin white horizontal lines across the middle, and two red dots. The windows can be dark or light. Use this to your advantage: a dark window on the sunlit side of the car, and a light window on the dark side—or the reverse, depending on the painting. A light car window standing out in a dark background is very dramatic.

You can use complementary colors to energize a passage (e.g. a red-orange car against a deep blue background). And if a car is red, add some orange or yellow to the mix to vary the color. Don't forget to leave parts of the car unpainted to give sparkle to the vehicle and suggest sunlight glinting off the metal surface. When painting a vehicle by itself, make a pen-and-ink contour sketch before adding bright colors.

Cars are a good subject to practice on. I have drawn many vehicles while waiting in a parking lot. It's challenging to capture all the complex curves and foreshortening effects; sitting in a parking lot gives you plenty of options to choose from. Here are a few examples.

ELYSIAN PARK BRIDGE In this sketch, I left the windows dark, used a bright color for each car, and made sure the brake lights were "on" to give the piece a nice red accent.

RUSH HOUR, LOS ANGELES Study the vehicles in this scene to see how simply they are rendered: two horizontal rectangles with white lines across the top edge of each, two dark spots along the bottom to represent tires, with two bright red dots just above for the brake lights.

CHINATOWN I used varying line weights to give these vehicles interest. Because they are general carlike shapes positioned in an urban setting, the eye accepts them as vehicles, even though they are very rough.

KAUAI OUTFITTERS This started as a quick contour pen sketch which I painted later in the studio.

VIEW FROM THE DECK Here is a quick study from a deck of two parked cars. If you always carry your sketchbook with you, you can practice drawing vehicles whenever you have a moment.

White Paint

Historically, traditional transparent watercolorists rely upon the white of the paper for all their whites and highlights. Some painters use frisket to reserve areas of pure white paper, allowing them to freely paint over an area. After the paint dries, they remove the frisket to expose the unpainted paper. While I have done that in the past, I prefer the selective use of white paint. Used with a good rigger brush, white paint can add the final flourish to a painting.

Rather than covering large areas, I use it for accent lines and final details: small tree branches, window mullions, railings, rafter tails, and other architectural details. I also use it for signage and car headlights, and to suggest miscellaneous detail in a dark and distant background, as well as interior illumination in a building or house at night. Sometimes I lightly splatter white over a dark grouping of trees.

I have found that titanium white provides the best coverage. Be sure to use a light touch, however. A painting can go from bright and sparkly to overworked and chalky very quickly. Here are some examples.

CABINS AT CRYSTAL COVE This is primarily a dark painting with deep colors. I painted the window mullions and deck railings with white paint and a rigger brush to accent the architectural lines and add sparkle to the scene.

COLORADO RANCH HOUSE Because the porch is almost completely in shadow, I needed to define the doors and windows. While the windows and doorframes are not that bright in reality, I exaggerated the color so they would stand out and invite the viewer in. I also used white paint to accentuate the standing seam metal roof.

FOUR-LEVEL INTERCHANGE In addition to the headlights and reflections, I used white paint to give texture to the hazy sky. I also applied a light wash of white to the freeway structure to suggest a dim and dusky afternoon.

REDLANDS FIREWORKS I had to depict fireworks in this scene. After painting the sky dark ultramarine blue, I added drops of white paint, letting them blossom and spread at random. Once dry, I painted a few streaks of white by smearing tiny drops of paint with my finger.

RIVERBOAT This riverboat is surrounded by bright white railing. In addition, I used white paint for the mullions and the dimensional letters between the smokestacks.

Night Scenes

Night paintings mean dramatic and unexpected scenes. The environment has a completely different color palette after the sun goes down. Everything has a cool, dark blue-and-gray tone. Light from streetlights and building windows creates a glow of warm colors emanating from the source. The night sky is darkest at the top of the page and lightens as it nears the horizon, due to reflected light.

One good way to gain an understanding of how light works at night is to take photos at night.

For my night scenes, I paint an underwash of glowing yellow, starting at the main source of light, and gradually adding red and blue as I move away from the source. Use opaque white to highlight windows and other random details. Finally, remember to think simply in terms of composition and keep detail to a minimum. Here are a few examples.

DOROTHY CHANDLER PAVILION Light glows from the entrance of this concert venue and colors reflect onto the plaza paving. People are mere specks of paint in different colors.

PASADENA CIVIC AUDITORIUM The gradated wash of raw sienna to alizarin crimson to ultramarine blue is clearly visible in this scene. I used marine blue with burnt umber to make the night sky dark.

COLORADO STREET BRIDGE, MOONLIGHT In this painting, I covered the entire sheet with a dark wash of blue and purple, leaving an unpainted area for the moon. When the background wash dried, I added heavy layers of green, blue, and yellow to define the bridge and trees.

CHURCH, JACKSON SQUARE, NEW ORLEANS
This night scene is dramatic, as the sky is not yet dark. The church is silhouetted in dark, with only the windows lit. A crowd gathers at the brightly illuminated entrance.

CARGO SHIP, PENSACOLA, FLORIDA
The sky is very dark. The ship is defined with illuminated windows and white paint that suggests machinery and action on the deck.

Interiors

Interiors are always an interesting subject to sketch in watercolor. Many of us are inside much of the time, and this is the perfect way to gain practice in a comfortable environment. I have filled many sketchbook pages with scenes of train stations, airports, meetings, and waiting rooms, and from my seat in both trains and planes.

One of the key challenges with interiors is perspective, and the simplest kind of perspective is one-point perspective. (See pages 30-31.) In one-point perspective, all lines converge to a single vanishing point, like looking down a long railroad track.

The second challenge is lighting. After preparing my initial sketch, I usually do a gradated wash over the entire sketch, starting at the primary light source (usually a window) with pale yellow and moving to the outer edges of the sketch, adding red and blue as the light dissipates. The color changes from warm to cool.

With a solid perspective sketch and a gradated warm-to-cool wash, all that remains is the addition of architectural accents and details—and perhaps a few people to complete the painting. Shown here are a few examples.

LOS ANGELES UNION STATION Demonstrated here is one-point perspective with two light sources: the side windows, where morning light is streaming in, and the entrance to the concourse at the far end of the hall. Notice that the light and people are reflected in the floor tiles.

INDOOR CONCERT I blocked in the floor and stadium seating quickly and without any detail. The people are a series of loose, blobular shapes sketched in a grid. Light comes from the stage and moves outward. This is a loose but effective method.

SHOPPING ARCADE, LOS ANGELES This is a colorful, one-point perspective of people, shops, signs, and umbrellas. Pedestrian bridges and a roof skylight create interest in this scene.

OPTOMETRIST OFFICE Demonstrated here is a flat, elevation-like sketch with no perspective. A colorful background and positive/negative painting make this an unusual piece.

SIGN SHOP, PASADENA This was done from a panoramic photo taken of a friend's workshop, and it's basically a pen sketch with paint added to select areas. The perspective has multiple vanishing points, due to the curves created by the panoramic photo.

Light Touch

Occasionally, I like to take a "light-touch" approach. With this technique, apply small amounts of pigment to dry paper and immediately soften with water. When used in an urban scene with architectural subjects, the effect is a bright sunny day. The white of the paper shines through and creates a soft glow of illumination.

This requires patience and a delicate hand. You will be tempted to apply much more paint than necessary. It's very easy to turn a bright, high-key painting into a dark and confused mess.

Don't worry about defining the edges throughout. After painting an area, touch a few select spots with water, and let the color bleed beyond the shape. When adding color to a pen sketch, let the color go beyond the lines in some places. The selective use of a water-soluble pen can help keep the sketch loose and light, as it will bleed when touched with water or paint. Here are a few examples.

PHILIPPE'S, LOS ANGELES Compare this version with the finished painting on page 117 and note how much softer and lighter this painting is. Some areas are almost out of focus, inviting the viewer to complete the painting in his or her imagination.

LOS ANGELES FROM CITY HALL I completed this painting on hot-pressed paper. The paint sits on the smooth surface, rather than soaking in. Each color is distinct, and there is little blending. Splashes of paint and clear water help keep this painting light.

KEELER TRAIN STATION I tried to keep the darks to a minimum in this sketch. Other than the two dark trees, most of the painting consists of one wash of light paint, which lets the sky and mountain color carry through into the building's shadow.

CABOOSE, SANTA FE, NEW MEXICO I used light pencil lines for this sketch. I applied colors in a single wash, allowing them to blend together, and leaving the edges undefined.

SANTA FE TRAIN STATION In this sketch, the sky color carries over into the building's shadows. Most of the station has blurry, "lost" edges, particularly where the roof meets the sky.

Positive & Negative Painting

Negative painting occurs when you paint around a shape with a dark color to define the lighter-value object. You can use this technique to define tree trunks and branches, architectural details, cars, and people. You can also create interesting designs and patterns by placing positive and negative passages together. I like to have a tree trunk go from negative to positive and back to negative, depending on the background value.

This back-and-forth also works for bridge railings painted with dark values against a white cloud and reversed out (or negatively painted) against deep blue sky.

Another example are window mullions. Windows sometimes appear dark against a light building, so I paint the mullions with white paint. Windows also can reflect sky and trees and have both light and dark values in each window. In that instance, I use white paint for mullions over a dark window and dark paint where lighter values are reflected.

Forcing the contrast in these positive/negative areas creates a lot of interest in a small space and suggests intricate detail where there is none. Here are a few examples.

WOODEN BRIDGE, LANGHAM HUNTINGTON The interplay of positive and negative lines and shapes really makes this painting work. Notice how the bridge structure is reversed out from the dark foliage and becomes dark when it reaches the sky. The palm fronds are also both dark and light, depending on what's behind them.

WINE BAR This little study started with a line drawing, to which I applied a dark-to-light wash. I then painted each wine bottle, either as a positive shape or a negative shape defined by painting around the bottle with a dark value.

GARDEN STEPS, PASADENA You can see clearly how both positive and negative line work help communicate the sense of a forest and distant light. Notice how the trunks and branches go from dark to light to dark.

OLVERA STREET MARIACHIS Most of this sketch is painted negatively. The dark background unifies the scene and allows the gazebo, people, and balloons to stand out with bold colors and highlights.

IN-N-OUT BURGER I only had time for a three-minute sketch as I was waiting in my car for a burger. Later that night in my studio, I realized I had nothing more than an abstract series of lines and some vague shapes indicating the outline of a car and the sign. That forced me to apply color and value boldly, disregarding the notion of realism and aiming for a pure graphic statement.

Demonstrations

Painting Night Scenes

The building in this demonstration, Vista del Arroyo, is a historic building overlooking the arroyo in Pasadena, California. It's surrounded by trees and has interesting shadow patterns during the day and dramatic lighting at night.

COMPOSITION & COLOR STUDIES

Begin with a rough study. Here I created a pencil sketch based on my daytime reference, when one part of the building casts a distinctive shadow across the opposite wall. I also created a pen-and-ink study of the building at night.

tip

YOU DON'T HAVE TO FOLLOW YOUR REFERENCE IMAGES PRECISELY; EMPHASIZE AND IMAGINE LIGHT COMING FROM DIFFERENT SOURCES TO ADD DRAMA.

CHOOSING TIME OF DAY

The same location can look vastly different depending on the time of day. To help decide what time of day to paint your scene, visit the location at different times and take multiple reference photos. Create rough sketches and color studies for both the daytime and nighttime scenes, and choose the one that speaks to you.

INITIAL DRAWING

Create your drawing in three stages. First block everything out using a soft pencil, making sure the proportions and composition are correct. Then go over the pencil sketch with a waterproof, fine-point pen, adding details, tree shapes, and the grid of windows. Finish by accenting some of the lines and shapes with a water-soluble pen, which will bleed when you add paint.

BACKGROUND WASHES

To create the look of light emanating from the center of the building, apply a series of glazing washes using gamboge nova, fading to alizarin crimson and ultramarine blue. Start with dry paper and place the colors adjacent to each other so they blend on the paper.

Increase the amount of color in each wash, letting each glaze dry before painting the next. Lay down at least three washes, leaving a bit of white paper in the very center.

SURROUNDING TREES

As soon as the background washes dry, block in the tree shapes. Rather than trying to paint individual trees, paint an abstract wash that loosely represents tree shapes with a variety of blues, greens, and yellows, plus a touch of red and orange accents.

ADDING DEPTH

Continue adding layers of paint to the trees, making the dark areas darker and keeping the light areas light. Use greenish-yellow for the trees nearest the light of the building. Add shadows to the outer walls and upper face of the building using cobalt blue and opera, letting the paint mix and blend on the paper. As you work, use the chisel end of a brush to scrape out random tree trunks and branches.

THE FINAL DETAILS

Paint the roof bright red to provide a complementary color accent, and add more color and texture to the walls with cobalt blue, opera, and a touch of raw sienna. Using titanium white and a rigger brush, suggest windows lit from within and sketch in a few more tree trunks and branches. Using the same brush, paint some of the windows dark, and extend some of the white branches with dark paint.

Painting a Traditional Still Life

Setting up a traditional still life is as easy as pouring some wine, cutting a few slices of cheese, and arranging the elements outside with some afternoon sun creating a nice cast shadow. I moved everything around until I was pleased with the composition and then took several photos before rearranging them to get a different shadow pattern. I liked this arrangement the best.

STUDY SKETCH & INITIAL DRAWING

Roughly sketch the scene in pencil first to establish the big shapes. I used a 9" x 12" multimedia sketchbook and both waterproof and water-soluble pens.

Once you're happy with the sketch, create the initial drawing for your final painting. Block out the objects in pencil before sketching over them with pen. I was careful to capture the symmetry of the bottle and glass and tried to get the perspective right. I wanted the drawing to be loose and sketchy, so I used a loose grip on my pen and many delicate lines to establish the forms.

WINE BOTTLE

Paint the wine bottle with one wash of ultramarine blue, burnt umber, phthalo blue, and olive green. For the black top, use ultramarine blue and burnt umber with very little water. Leave a vertical area unpainted to suggest a highlight. At the base, paint the shadow with a mixture of ultramarine blue and alizarin crimson, letting the colors mix together on the paper. Soften the top edge of the shadow and the top of the bottle with clear water. Paint the label graphic with raw sienna and quinacridone gold.

WINE GLASS

Paint the wine in the glass with alizarin crimson, varying the intensity of color to give it some interest. Leave a thin edge unpainted to suggest the highlight along the surface of the wine and on the highlighted side of the glass. Paint the glass stem and shadow with ultramarine blue and alizarin crimson.

CHEESE SLICES

Use a mixture of new gamboge, quinacridone gold, and raw sienna to paint the cheese shapes and cork, leaving a few small spots of unpainted paper. While the paint is still wet, block in the shadows with cobalt blue and opera, letting the colors mix on the paper. Vary the ratio of colors as you paint the cutting board's shadow, and add water to soften the edges.

CUTTING BOARD & KNIFE

After the shadow color is dry, paint the cutting board with a combination of burnt sienna, raw sienna, and quinacridone gold. Use raw sienna to suggest the table, letting the color drop back to white paper to create a vignette. Use a light touch to drop in cadmium red light on the top and side of the knife. Use burnt sienna to paint the shadows on the cheese block and slices, paying attention to the cast shadows as well.

ENHANCEMENTS & FINAL TOUCHES

Deepen the wine color with ultramarine blue, and add a cast shadow across the wine label with a light mixture of cobalt blue and opera. Add some more red to the knife. Go over the label and cheese board lettering with ultramarine blue and burnt umber and a rigger brush, smearing the letters with drops of clear water. Use that same color to enhance the wine label graphics. Use a rigger brush and titanium white to add the curve of reflected light on the underside of the wine glass as well as the logo on the knife and highlights on the corkscrew, knife blade, and knife loop. Finish with a few splashes of paint.

Taking Artistic License

Trail Ridge Road is a beautiful drive through Rocky Mountain National Park in Colorado, with scenic vistas around every turn. This view is from a small parking area overlooking a valley. You can see the road as it climbs up the mountainside and winds its way through the forest. I love this view, but it is a little monochromatic. I want to spice it up a bit. Even when working from reference photographs, remember that you don't have to stay completely true to the reference. Use artistic license to make tweaks and adjustments to add drama, color, or dimension.

STUDY SKETCHES

Start with a pencil value study, establishing the dark, medium, and light areas of the scene.

tip

IF YOU'RE OUT SOMEWHERE AND DON'T HAVE TIME TO CREATE A VALUE OR COMPOSITION STUDY ON LOCATION, MAKE A QUICK PEN SKETCH AND TAKE A PHOTO.

Create a couple of color studies: one looser and one tighter. This will help you refamiliarize yourself with the scene and is a good warm-up.

INITIAL DRAWING

For the drawing, block everything out with a soft pencil. Then go over the pencil sketch with a waterproof, fine-point pen, and accent the mountain shapes and major design lines with a water-soluble pen.

FIRST WASH

Begin painting with the sky with ultramarine, cobalt, and cerulean blue, with a touch of burnt umber to create gray cloud shadows suggesting a storm. The water-soluble pen adds dark energy and drama to the clouds.

MOUNTAINS

While the sky dries, paint the distant mountains with a mixture of ultramarine blue and alizarin crimson. Using marine blue, burnt sienna, and new gamboge, block in the next range of mountains, letting it blend with the purple in spots. Leave a few thin lines unpainted where one mountain crosses in front of the other, and vary the paint density and color to create texture and interest.

VALLEY COLORS & FOREGROUND

Paint the valley as if it were full of aspen trees, using new gamboge and permanent yellow orange. The bleeding pen blurs the pine tree shapes and lines. Finish the first wash by laying in the green meadows with a mixture of marine blue mixed with burnt sienna, olive green, and greenish yellow.

PINE TREES & SHADOWS

Using marine blue, ultramarine blue, burnt sienna, and burnt umber, add the pine tree forests on the valley floor and distant mountain. Use a medium-sized sable brush to block in larger masses of trees, suggesting the tips with the point of the brush and occasionally using a rigger to delineate trunks and branches on the foreground trees.

CREATING DEPTH

Further define the mountains with another application of deep green-blue to create depth and articulate the foreground mountains. Add more darks to the sky, allowing the clouds to stand out more clearly.

THE FINAL DETAILS

Use a rigger pen and titanium white to add texture to the denser parts of the pine tree forests. Add touches of cadmium red light to suggest the occasional cabin, vehicle, or hiker. Finish by extending the left side of the triangular mountain to reduce its symmetry and punch up some of the dark shadow areas.

Painting Urban Scenes

This painting is one of my favorite restaurants in downtown Los Angeles. My reference photo was taken from across the street and captures all the elements essential for a gritty urban scene: signage, phone poles, wires, billboards, people, and reflections. This photo also includes some vehicles and a small tree, but I chose to eliminate them to focus on the building, people, and shadows. Remember—artistic license!

VALUE & COLOR STUDIES

Start with a simple value study in pencil. Here, I altered the shadow pattern to create more interest, putting the background building in shadow to emphasize the foreground, and imagining the awnings casting an angular shadow across the wall. To push the values even further, create a second value study with pen and ink. From these value and composition explorations, do a color study. These preliminary steps help you warm up.

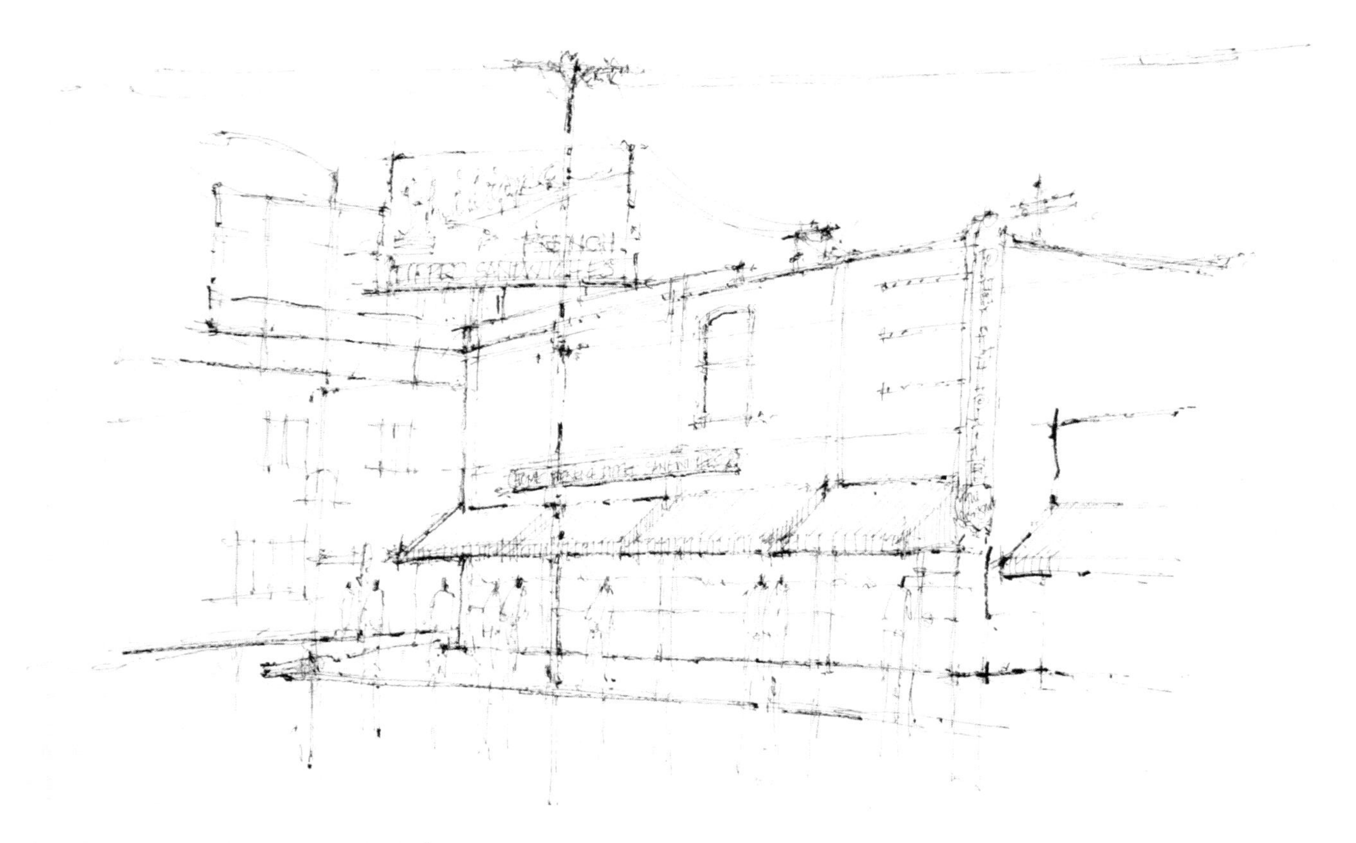

INITIAL DRAWING

Using both the photo reference and studies, block out the drawing lightly with pencil, making sure the perspective is correct and the phone pole isn't in the center of the scene. Keep the drawing small, leaving plenty of white space all around. This will allow you to vignette the scene (if you wish), and the white space also allows for last-minute recomposing if needed. Go over the pencil with pen, sketching over the lines with loose strokes and trying to keep the casual "urban sketch" feeling. Finally, accent key architectural lines and details with a water-soluble pen.

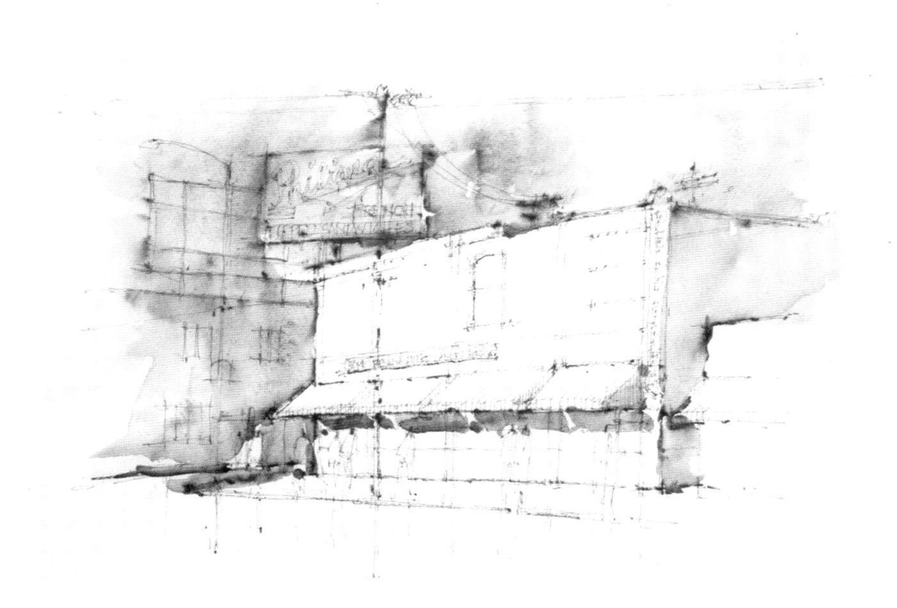

SKY & SHADOWS

Paint the sky using ultramarine blue, cobalt blue, raw sienna, and alizarin crimson. To unify the painting, pull the sky color into the building shadows. Use this same wash for the awning shadows.

WARM BUILDING TONES

Using raw sienna, paint a loose wash over the buildings and foreground. Stay casual with the paint application, letting there be variation in color and texture to suggest sunlight and warmth. Notice how the water-soluble pen bleeds and adds some random messiness to the scene.

ENHANCED SHADOWS

Paint another wash of ultramarine blue and alizarin crimson in the building shadow areas, allowing the colors to mix on the paper as much as possible. Paint the sign with ultramarine blue and burnt umber, letting it blend with the billboard. Using those same colors, block in the windows and the building wall, making sure to pull down the colors to suggest reflections in the sidewalk and street. Leave some unpainted areas for the people, and use a rigger brush and a light wash of warm gray to suggest the stripes on the awnings.

SIGNS & PEOPLE

Using cadmium red light, permanent yellow orange, and gamboge nova, paint the tall vertical sign. Notice how the colors blend from red at the top to yellow at the bottom. Paint the edge of the sign with cobalt turquoise light. To make the people bright accents in the scene, paint them with pure pigment, being sure to add the reflections in the sidewalk and street. Add some cerulean blue to the windows of the background building.

MORE CONTRAST

Add dark blue to the window and dark brown to the architectural band along the bottom half of the wall to create additional contrast in the scene.

OUTLINES

Using titanium white and a rigger brush, paint the signage and outline the windows and doors. Suggest a few frame lines on the backside of the billboard. Note that if some of the signage text is in color it must be painted white first to create a clean base for new color.

THE FINAL DETAILS

Paint the yellow signage text again with new gamboge and add in the red, orange, and teal accent stripes. Outline the single window with titanium white, and suggest some power lines with dark gray paint and a rigger brush. Paint the power lines white where they cross a dark area. Finally, add a red curb in front of the building.

Painting Still Lifes

Like many, I am a collector of art supplies. I enjoy the tools and equipment just as I enjoy the process of drawing and painting, and they make an excellent subject for a still life. This scene features my favorite paint box with various tubes of paint scattered about the table. Everything is placed on my worktable, with a strong light from the left creating a nice shadow across the scene. Set up your own still life with your favorite supplies, or work from my photo reference.

VALUE & COLOR STUDIES

Start with a quick composition and value study in pencil, establishing a nice shadow pattern. Next to the sketch, do a color study, blocking it out first in pencil, and adding some pen work before painting it. This is just a warm-up sketch to look at the scene and get a feel for the colors and the way you'd like them to blend. If needed, you can do more than one color study.

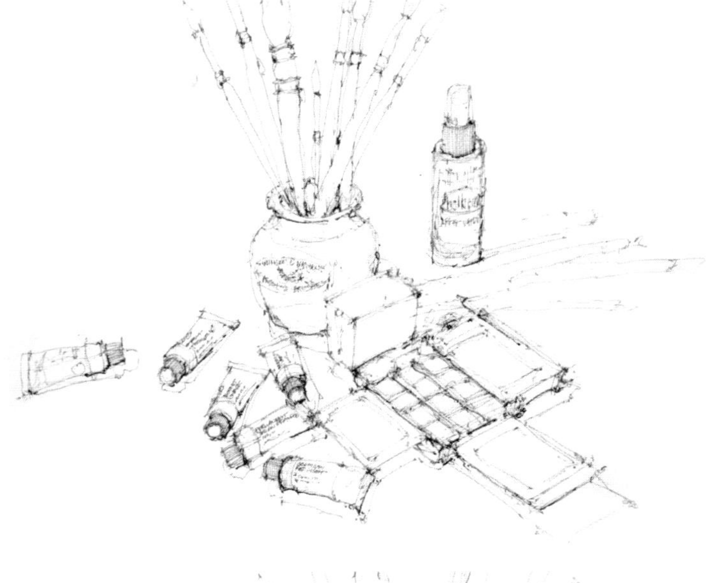

INITIAL DRAWING

Even with the actual subject before you, use your study sketch and photo reference as you create the initial drawing. Using pencil and both waterproof and water-soluble pens, block in the forms. Aim to capture all the good aspects of the initial sketches, but if you try to copy your studies exactly, the final work may look stiff and lack energy. Instead, use the initial work as inspiration, and try to let the final drawing have a life of its own.

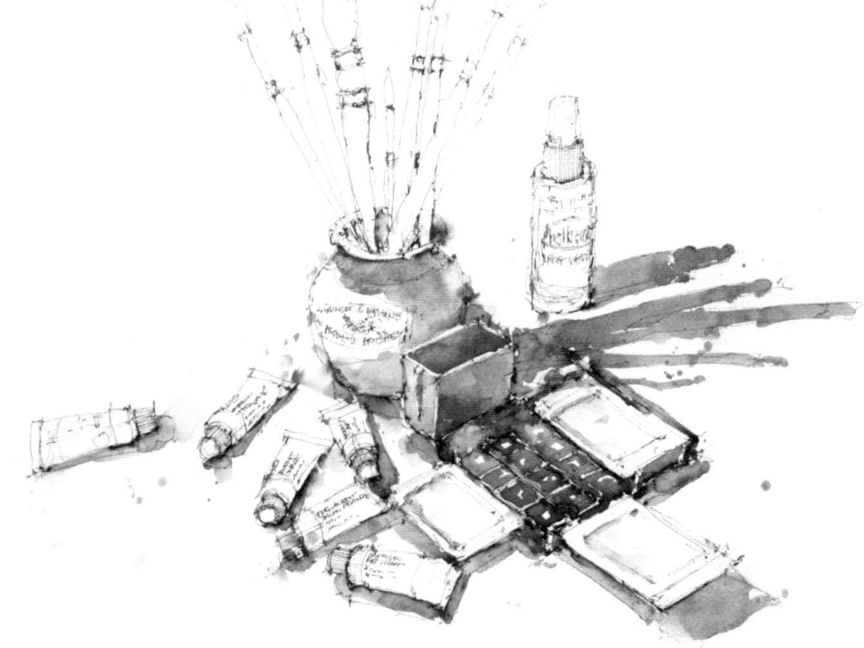

COLOR & SHADOW

Start with the paint box for the first wash. Use ultramarine blue, leaving the highlights on the water cup unpainted. While the paint is still wet, add the paint pans, taking care to leave a touch of white paper showing through to suggest reflected light on wet paint. Using ultramarine blue with a bit of alizarin crimson, suggest the mixing areas by painting the shadowed edges.

Paint the cast shadows with a mixture of ultramarine blue and alizarin crimson, letting the shadow blend with the brush holder color to eliminate the hard edge. Accentuate the brush cast shadows, letting them spread across the scene dramatically to create movement. Add little shadows under each paint tube and the spray bottle.

BRUSHES

The brushes add both movement and color to the scene, and the key is to render them loosely with as little detail as possible. Paint the handles, taking care to leave a narrow unpainted line to suggest a highlight on each one. Apply a touch of clear water to selected areas to bleed the color into the background. Let the brush colors blend together where they cross, and darken the brush holder shadows with a mixture of ultramarine blue and burnt umber.

PAINT TUBES

The paint tubes are simple and easy to paint, but it's important to pay attention to a few details. Leave a small line of white paper within the color band to suggest a highlight. It's better to leave this unpainted. Add just a touch of gray to the shadowed side and where the tube is crimped. Don't overdo this—subtle is better. Use that same gray to paint the tube cap, remembering to leave the highlight side unpainted.

BACKGROUND & FINAL TOUCHES

Use raw sienna to paint the table surface and background. While you may be tempted to paint a smooth, even wash, vary the amount of paint and water to create light and dark areas. Paint right over the shadows, and bring some color into the brush holder and spray bottle to warm them up. The brush holder will look white as soon as you add color to the table beyond. Add a few touches of white paint to the paint box and spray bottle. Lightly splash some paint over everything to finish it up and add energy.

Painting Interior Scenes

I love trains, and living in Los Angeles with both friends and projects in San Diego means that I have a good excuse to ride one. This is the waiting room in the Santa Fe Depot in downtown San Diego on a sunny afternoon. Painting an interior scene is similar to painting a night scene, with a gradated wash of light to dark values as a background for the rest of the painting. I want light coming from the far windows, illuminating the waiting room and reflecting on the floor.

LOCATION SKETCH & PAINTING PRACTICE

If possible, do a location sketch first. Establish a vanishing point, and draw radiating lines coming out from the center. You can see the guidelines in my sketch here. Block out the rest of the scene using these guidelines, paying attention to the arches and ceiling curves and how they get smaller and closer together as they recede. For this kind of scene, I refer to my location sketch rather than a photograph—note how the light pattern is very static and harsh in the photo.

INITIAL DRAWING & BACKGROUND WASHES

Referring to your sketch, locate the vanishing point, and block out the perspective lines. Draw in the back ticketing wall and curved roof at the far end. Once you're pleased with the proportions, draw the series of curved ceiling and wall archways. Then draw a horizontal line through the vanishing point to locate the heads of all the passengers. It's important to note that no matter how far apart people are standing, their heads will generally align. Go over the pencil sketch with a waterproof, fine-point pen, adding details, light fixtures, and the windows. Accent some of the lines and shapes with a water-soluble pen, which will bleed when you add paint.

The light in the study sketch comes from the center of the far window. Paint a series of washes using new gamboge and raw sienna at the center, fading into alizarin crimson and ultramarine blue at the edges. Start with dry paper and place the colors adjacent to each other so they blend on the paper. I did two washes, increasing the amount of color each time, letting each glaze dry before painting the next. Leave the paper white in the center.

CEILING ARCHES

Use ultramarine blue and alizarin crimson to define the ceiling arches on the third wash. Keep it loose and watery, letting the pigments blend on the paper. Add burnt umber to the ceiling, using distinct brushstrokes to suggest dark wood beams. The background wash of gradating color helps unify the painting and suggests soft illumination.

PEOPLE & REFLECTIONS

Use a variety of bold accent colors to block in the people. I exaggerated and adjusted the colors to keep the painting bright and lively. Where two people are close to each other, allow the colors to blend together. Extend the colors down into the floor to suggest reflections on the shiny tile. Notice that the light from the far window also reflects in the floor.

BACKGROUND DEPTH & LIGHT FIXTURES

Paint the ticketing counter with a dark mixture of ultramarine blue and burnt umber to create depth and help the figures stand out. Leave a slight edge of unpainted paper around some of the heads. Use a lighter mixture of the same color to paint the light fixtures and the archways in the wall. Then use a rigger brush to define the chains holding the lights. Use titanium white to paint the lights. Using a darker application of burnt umber, punch up some of the ceiling beams, and add mullions to the doors on the left.

ENHANCEMENTS & FINAL DETAILS

Finish by using a rigger brush and titanium white paint to add tile lines in the floor and mullion lines in the inside archways. Clarify the vertical columns, being sure to reflect that shape in the floor. Finally, add a few white accents to the passengers, suggesting the occasional white shirt.

Final Thoughts

Start on the right track by being organized. It will pay off in the long run. Get in the habit of signing and photographing all your work. Additionally, keep notes of all your workshop and demonstration experiences. Whether I attend an evening demonstration or a multi-day workshop, I take and keep thorough notes and store them in three-ring binders so they are easy to access.

Set up your infrastructure to paint in a limited number of paper sizes. I recommend one-quarter, one-half, and full-size sheets. Have boards trimmed to these sizes on which you can clip your papers. It's easier (and cost effective) to frame your work with limited frame sizes.

Design a simple business card, and attach it to the back of all your framed pieces. That way it's easy for your customers to find your information again or recommend you to their friends.

GOOD HABITS TO DEVELOP

DISCIPLINE Sketch and paint even when you don't feel like it. I've heard that the harder you work, the luckier you get. New York artist Chuck Close said, "Inspiration is for amateurs. The rest of us just get to work."

QUALITY Strive to do your best work all the time.

QUANTITY Paint a lot. Try to draw or paint each day. It's like golf, tennis, or piano. Practice makes all the difference. I frequently redo a painting until it looks like I just whipped it out. I want my work to look like I enjoyed the process.

SKETCHBOOK WORK Constant sketchbook work is invaluable in the development of a good painter.

MIXING Mix the paint on the paper, and use an uncomfortably big brush.

LOCATION PAINTING Work from life whenever possible. Outside is best, but it's easy to set up a still life inside. Any subject can be an interesting sketch or painting.

READ Nothing is a substitute for the skills you develop while painting. You can, however, learn much from books, both from a technical and an inspirational standpoint. Build a good art library.

INSTRUCTION Take classes, seminars, and workshops from a variety of artists. Don't learn from just one teacher. But take instruction with a grain of salt. Ultimately, you should do what works for you.

Inspiration

Every day matters—we each only have few, so try to make each one count.

Watercolor painting is like jazz. A great painting has the structure of good composition and a solid value pattern, but within that structure are exciting improvisational notes and color passages.

Balance art with life; don't neglect time with friends or family.

Never let reality stand in the way of a good painting.

Your style will find you.

There is a built-in irony of the happy painter. It sometimes looks as if things are going smoothly as he or she sits in a grassy field playing with art materials, when in reality, it is a challenge and a struggle to wrestle each painting into submission.

Watercolor is a challenging medium. The difficulties are worth the rewards. Above all, remember to have fun on your journey.

About the Artist

Joseph Stoddard is a partner at SKA Design, an environmental graphics design office located in South Pasadena. He paints in the evenings and on weekends and is a frequent demonstrator and workshop teacher around Southern California.

Joseph has produced paintings for many Pasadena events, including the Bungalow Heaven Annual Tour, the Colorado Street Bridge Party, the Pasadena Showcase House of Design, the California Art Club Artists for Architecture Painting Project, the Pasadena Symphony, and the Pasadena Pops Orchestra. His work has been featured in *The Art of Watercolor*, a French art magazine; *Studios* magazine; and *Watercolor Artist* magazine. His studio was featured in *The Man Cave Book*.

Joseph's paintings have also appeared on the covers of a variety of publications, including *Westways Magazine*, *Pasadena Magazine*, a book series published by the Historical Society of Southern California, and the Lost and Found Series by Many Moons Press. In 2001, a book of his sketches entitled *Pasadena Sketchbook* was published, with a second edition published in 2008. Additionally, a collection of sketches of the University of Redlands entitled *Redlands Sketchbook* was published in 2007. Joseph is the author of *Expressive Color* (Quarto Publishing Group, 2008) and is currently working on a sketchbook about Los Angeles and a series of new paintings for the third edition of *Pasadena Sketchbook*.

To see more of Joseph's work, visit www.josephstoddard.com.